What We Now Know About Race and Ethnicity

What We Now Know About Race and Ethnicity

Michael Banton

berghahn
NEW YORK · OXFORD
www.berghahnbooks.com

Published by

Berghahn Books

www.berghahnbooks.com

Library of Congress Cataloging-in-Publication Data

Banton, Michael, 1926–
   What we now know about race and ethnicity / by Michael Banton.
      pages cm
   Includes bibliographical references and index.
   ISBN 978-1-78238-603-2 (hardback : alk. paper) —
   ISBN 978-1-78238-717-6 (paperback. : alk. paper) —
   ISBN 978-1-78238-613-1 (ebook)
   1. Race. 2. Ethnicity. 3. Ethnicity—United States. 4. United States—Race
relations. I. Title.
   HT1521.B354 2015
   305.8—dc23

                                                            2015006532

British Library Cataloguing in Publication Data

A catalogue record for this book is available from the British Library

ISBN 978-1-78238-603-2 (hardback)
ISBN 978-1-78238-717-6 (paperback)
ISBN 978-1-78238-613-1 (ebook)

Contents

Preface

Anyone who opens this book will already know a lot about 'race' and 'ethnicity'. They are words heard on television, read in newspapers and used in conversation. What the words mean will usually be clear from the context in which they are employed. Yet, because it is not always easy to distinguish between words and things, people sometimes wonder what race (or ethnicity) actually is. This book tries to resolve some of the confusion by distinguishing between the words' meanings in the popular or practical language of everyday life, and attempts to sharpen their meanings (or supersede use of them altogether) in technical or scientific language.

So there is more than one kind of knowledge. While we – all of us – know about the place of 'race' and 'ethnicity' in the practical sphere, this is not the end of the story. What specialists have learned in the past two hundred years or so about when and why racial and ethnic distinctions have become socially important is a different kind of knowledge, even if the two kinds can overlap. There may never be final answers to all the questions, but hopefully the nature of the underlying difficulties will have been clarified by the end of this book.

Many of the academic books about race and ethnicity that have been written by authors in the United States are prefaced by lists of the seminars and conferences at which portions of the work have been presented, exposing the arguments to beneficial criticism. The authors acknowledge the financial support of institutions, and, almost invariably, the contributions of many friends and colleagues who have helped them polish their texts. This is not that kind of book. The manuscript has been prepared in relative isolation and without any kind of grant. The stimulus for it – which came to me in June 2013 – has been the reaction of other specialists in the study of racial and ethnic relations who either reject or do not understand the philosophical presuppositions that underlie my recent writing. This impulse has been coupled with a desire to address colleagues in the United States. To me, very many of them seem so concerned with the political aspects of the black-white division in their own country that they do not reflect sufficiently on what they might learn from a European perspective.

Michael Banton
Downe, Kent

The Paradox

In 2002 the American Sociological Association (ASA) formally noted:

> Some scholarly and civic leaders believe that the very idea of 'race' has the effect of promoting social division and they have proposed that the government stop collecting these data altogether. Respected voices from the fields of human molecular biology and physical anthropology (supported by research from the Human Genome Project) assert that the concept of race has no validity in their respective fields.[1]

This may have been a reference to the statement issued by the American Association of Physical Anthropologists that declared, among other things, that 'there is no national, religious, linguistic or cultural group or economic class that constitutes a race'.[2]

The ASA statement continued: 'Growing numbers of humanist scholars, social anthropologists, and political commentators have joined the chorus in urging the nation to rid itself of the concept of race.' One scholar was quoted as saying that 'identifying people by race only deepens the racial divide'. The ASA thereby recognized an intellectual challenge. Scholars in several different fields were asking the ASA to help supersede an obsolete expression earlier advanced for the identification of certain kinds of biological difference.

The Association was in a fix. There was an intellectual issue and a political issue, for it was urged to respond to a proposal to forbid the California state government from collecting information on race and ethnicity.[3] Understandably, the political issue was given priority because a professional association can take a vote on a proposal of this kind, whereas an intellectual issue is better addressed by debate in academic books, journal articles and seminars.

So the Association issued an official statement on the 'Importance of Collecting Data on Race'. It maintained that such data should be collected because they were needed for the monitoring of social policies in the United States. There was no reference to ethnicity or to any 'racial divide' other than that between blacks and whites. The Association did not seize the opportunity to remind interested persons that, as a party to the International Convention on the Elimination of Racial Discrimination (ICERD), the United States had, since 1994, been under a treaty obligation to monitor and report to the Secretary-General of the United Nations about any inequalities affecting racial and ethnic groups within its population.

The position adopted by the ASA was paradoxical in that it combined two contradictory elements: a recognition that race no longer had any validity in the academic field within which it originated together with a defence of procedures which implied the opposite.

Its response was reactive, neglecting the opportunity to comment on the basis on which population data are collected. The US census of 2000 had introduced an important change when (in Question 6) it asked, 'What is this person's race? Mark one or more races to indicate what this person considers himself/herself to be'; this was followed by fifteen tick boxes. This momentous change, however, had come about by accident! A former director of the Census Bureau has reported that it was an 'anomaly' that had been left on the form 'inadvertently'.[4] The same question was then repeated in 2010. The old 'one-drop rule' required that many persons be classed as either black or white, and that a single drop of black 'blood' made that person black. Today, in the United States, there are many persons who value more than one line of descent and do not wish to be identified by one alone. How their wishes are to be respected, and data on the national population to be collected, is a political decision to be taken by the federal government and other authorities (including the Office of Management and Budget). The ASA, as a non-political body, could have offered its advice on the alternative possibilities. Instead, its statement endorsed the existing procedures.

The usage that the ASA defended was one peculiar to the United States. It addressed, not the concept of race, but the practice by which blacks in that country were identified by the one-drop rule; this is a peculiar mode of classification that is not applied to any other social category in the United States and is unknown outside that country. If some other mode of classification was sought, what should it be? In censuses within the United Kingdom of Great Britain and Northern Ireland people have been asked, 'What is your ethnic group?' and offered choices that used words like 'white' and 'mixed'. This last word is questionable, for everyone's ancestry is in some degree mixed. Some persons may not identify with an ethnic group for any purpose other than that of completing the census form. The reality is not one of 'groups', but of social categories. The practical challenge confronting the ASA was the greater because the ordinary English-language vocabulary encourages categorizations like 'mixed' even though they are misleading and can be offensive. Since this particular contrast implies that the unmixed are purer than the mixed, it is morally objectionable as well as scientifically indefensible.

For several reasons the intellectual challenge was, and remains, more difficult than the political challenge. One of them is that states have obligations under international law that require them to use the words 'race' and 'racial'. The perception of a conflict between scientific knowledge and public practice has arisen because scientists and legislators have different objectives and use different vocabularies in order to attain them. The scientists say, in effect, that 'once some of our predecessors thought that race might be a useful concept in biology; now we know that there is no place for such a word in our vocabulary'. The legislators say, in effect, that 'we know that the word race has misleading associations that we hope to dispel by educational measures, but at the present time its use is necessary to the discharge of our international and domestic obligations'.

It is instructive to reflect upon the paradoxical aspect of the ASA statement because it casts light on a general intellectual problem confronting the contemporary social sciences. It will be argued here that the only way to resolve the paradox is to distinguish two kinds of knowledge, practical and theoretical. In them, the most important words are used in different ways because they serve different purposes. For this reason, the argument has to be philosophical as well as sociological. It challenges today's sociologists to reconsider some of their fundamental assumptions. They will not easily be persuaded that there is such a paradox, that it calls for resolution, or that this is the only way to resolve it.

Yet in some respects the argument demands only a reorientation of what has been known for more than a century. The British perspective may differ slightly from that in the United States because British universities often have separate departments for the study of sociology and for the study of social policy. There is active interchange between the two fields, sometimes in the form of an exchange between pure and applied sociology, and when it comes to writing about 'race', many sociologists continually prefer to address social policy issues even though the sociological theory applicable in this field needs their attention.

A prime example of how pure social research advances beyond applied research is Emile Durkheim's famous study of the causes of suicide. It demonstrated the value of distinctively sociological inquiry. In the course of his study Durkheim referred no less than sixteen times to the work of one of his predecessors, Henry Morselli. Many readers would be astonished to discover how much Durkheim's book owed to Morselli's forty-nine numbered tables, quite apart from the unnumbered ones. Durkheim's thirty-two tables recapitulated Morselli's sequence, updating and occasionally elaborating his tables. The two authors considered the same possible contributory causes: climate, seasons, time of day, population density, mental illness, sex, race, religion, occupation, marital status, etc. They employed the same method of eliminating postulated causes.

The difference between them is that Morselli's impressive book was prepared as a contribution to social policy; it concluded that the 'social calamity' of suicide might be mitigated by giving 'force and energy to the moral character' and by achieving a better 'balance between individual needs and social utility'. Durkheim's intent was signalled by his subtitle, 'A Study in Sociology'. He elaborated a new and exciting set of ideas well summarized in an article by Barclay Johnson on 'Durkheim's One Cause of Suicide'.[5] By his analysis of the indicators of social integration, Durkheim uncovered a causal variable of which the individuals were not conscious. Morselli's book, though translated into English and German, has been forgotten. Durkheim's book, despite its occasional errors, has been a continuing inspiration to psychiatrists and to policy makers concerned with questions of social cohesion and integration. It is a basic text in sociology. A study that was not directed to short-term concerns has proved of profound value for the long-term.

The distinction between practical and theoretical knowledge helps resolve some of the misunderstandings that arise when the same word is used with different meanings. The study of social policy has to be rooted in the prevailing body of practical knowledge because its recommendations have to be addressed to policy makers and to the general public. It has to use ordinary language and to allow for the difficulties that can arise from its ambiguities. Thus words like 'anti-Semitism', 'Islamophobia', 'multiculturalism', 'race' and 'racism' are currently vital to the designation of kinds of social relations that people wish to promote and the attitudes they wish to oppose. Such words are used with many different meanings; their significance changes over time.

It is relatively easy to find a research problem in the field of public policy because the mass media highlight matters of public concern every day. Many sociologists choose to address policy issues, often those that have a particular reference to forms of inequality. In the United States they have focused on changes in the relations between immigrants and those already settled, against a background that stresses the imperatives of a democratic society. In the United Kingdom much teaching and research has analysed the regulation of immigration and the processes of settlement. Ordinary language suffices for most such studies.

Other sociologists try to answer specific questions chosen as part of a general exploration of the underlying causes of social behaviour, looking at features common to humans everywhere, and at what distinguishes one society or one historical period from another. In this they resemble economists, who similarly search out commonalities and differences in varying kinds of markets, and psychologists, who examine characteristics of the human mind and the differences between the behaviour of humans and other kinds of animals. At the heart of the mainstream approach in any social science is the conception of an explanandum, an observation or research finding for which an account is sought. A theory helps the researcher to advance such an account in the form of an explanation (the explanans). However, many of the academics who have written about 'race' and 'ethnicity' have started from current English-language meanings of these words instead of from the intellectual problems that have to be resolved.

The researcher is more likely to make an original contribution to knowledge if he or she has found (or been given) a good problem on which to work. They are not easy to find. Though a Ph.D. candidate is expected to review the relevant literature outlining the work of predecessors and identify one or more traditions of inquiry, even successful candidates have been heard to say that 'it was only when I was writing my dissertation that I got a clear conception of what my problem was'. Different traditions prioritize different questions, so that if there is no agreement on the explanandum there can be no agreement on which is the best solution to the problem.

A good research problem is one that can lead to a reliable and interesting result. If the explanation is to have the vital quality of cogency, its terms have to be defined, and no term can be acceptably defined without agreement on the purpose for which a definition is wanted. This is the source of the difference between ordinary (or practical) language and theoretical language. In ordinary language, a definition has to facilitate communication in contexts in which fine distinctions or possible ambiguities may not be important. To ascertain the meaning of an ordinary language word, the inquirer looks it up in a dictionary and selects the most appropriate of the alternatives offered. In the development of theoretical explanations, it is the nature of the explanandum that decides which concepts and which definitions are useful to achieve a result. Concepts have to be fit for purpose, and the explanandum embodies the purpose.[6]

Ordinary language conceptions, being limited to particular times and places, have been called folk concepts; they have been contrasted with analytical concepts that seek to transcend any such limitations. However, a simpler formulation of the same distinction is one drawn by American anthropologists when they contrast emic and etic constructs. An everyday example of the difference is that when a patient goes to a doctor for treatment, he or she reports his or her symptoms in ordinary language using emic constructs. The doctor makes a diagnosis, drawing upon technical knowledge expressed in etic constructs. According to one encyclopaedia, emic constructs are accounts expressed in categories meaningful to members of the community under study, whereas etic constructs are accounts expressed in categories meaningful to the community of scientific observers.[7]

The emic/etic distinction identifies two kinds of vocabulary. In sociology, some expressions are candidates for inclusion as concepts in an etic vocabulary, such as reciprocity, relative deprivation, social mobility, socio-economic status, and so on, for their users strive to make them culture-free.

Much academic writing about race has concentrated on the potentially misleading features of the ordinary language – or emic – conception concerned with practical knowledge, and has neglected the distinction between explanandum and explanans. The chief intellectual problem is to account for human variation, physical and cultural; that is the explanandum. When addressing this problem, the notion of race has to be evaluated as part of an explanans, and its value within the body of theoretical knowledge that attempts to account for human variation has to be assessed.

There are therefore two kinds of answer to the question of what we now know about race and ethnicity. An answer in terms of practical knowledge would set out current knowledge about the meanings of these words and how they can be used for the formulation and implementation of public policy in one or more specific countries at the present time. It would not regard the conceptions of race and ethnicity as problematic. An answer in terms of theoretical knowledge – such as is offered in this book – must maintain that our knowledge of the present-day situation is deepened if we know how we have come by this knowledge, for it teaches lessons about how our knowledge has grown and continues to grow. It also explains why some lines of argument, though popular in their time, have been proven wrong. In particular, it considers whether the expressions 'race' and 'ethnicity' are fit for purpose: do they satisfactorily identify the behaviour that calls for explanation? An answer in these terms offers knowledge in greater depth.

The founding fathers of sociology set out to uncover underlying causes of social behaviour and proposed new concepts (like Durkheim's concept of anomie). They aimed to promote the growth of objective knowledge, that is to say knowledge that possesses the quality of cogency; such knowledge exists in a body of propositions that have to be accepted as valid by everyone who has a serious interest in the matter, including those who, because of their political commitments, are apprehensive about the possible implications of particular propositions.

One of the abiding problems of philosophy is that of the relation between things and words. The growth of theoretical knowledge depends upon a relation between the two that differs from the growth of practical knowledge. This opens a door to a resolution of the 2002 paradox. To set out this argument, it is necessary first to trace the history of how the paradox has arisen; then, second, to uncover the philosophical issues that underlie it. This demands, in chapters 1 and 2, summary histories of the sources of current conceptions of race and the many meanings the word has acquired, first in biology and then in social life. Some readers may be surprised by the contention that any history the word has in biology is only as a claim to explanatory value advanced at the beginning of the nineteenth century but demolished by its end. After the middle of the century, as Charles Darwin implicitly acknowledged, the popular meaning dominated use of the word. Chapter 2 has therefore to indicate the political moves that gave it such a special meaning in the United States. From the mid-twentieth century it has to do this against a backdrop of international law and politics, where the word 'race' has become increasingly important, as is outlined in chapter 3.

The reaction of many US sociologists in 2002 was to maintain that race, as 'a principal category in the organization of daily social life', was something quite separate from the possibility that it might be a biological category. Maybe it was separate for them, but that was no answer to the charge that its use in the United States promoted social division. Their argument that 'race as a social construct ... is central to societal organization' reinforced an over-simple belief about the relation between a social and a biological category, and it legitimated administrative practices that some of their members must, on political grounds, have considered in need of reform. The 'social construct' argument does not resolve the paradox. The only way to dismantle it, according to this book, is to build on the distinction between practical and theoretical knowledge.

Does this still matter? While this book was in preparation, a volume appeared from Princeton University Press under the title *Creating a New Racial Order: How Immigration, Multiracialism, Genomics, and the Young can Remake America*.[8] It was hailed by Henry Louis Gates, of Harvard University, as showing that 'racial order remains one of the most reliable ways of organizing our past and present as Americans'. Why should he write 'racial order' rather than 'social order'? Why should the authors, and their respected colleague, assume that 'racial' is the adjective that most correctly identifies the division they deplore? They recycle an obsolete and pernicious mode of thought.

The argument of the pages that follow is that one of the main tasks of social science is to discover better explanations of the social significance attributed to human physical differences, comparing the significance attributed to various phenotypical differences with other kinds of difference, both physical and social. As part of this task, it is necessary to consider how effective prevailing ideas of race and ethnicity are in accounting for those differences, and whether they can be improved upon. If they are in any way defective, how is it that they have they come into general use?

The main story has to start in the United States. In the nineteenth century whites in the US South referred to slavery as the 'peculiar institution'. This book contends that the popular but ill-considered conception of race that is bound up with the one-drop rule has become the new peculiar institution; it is peculiar both in being restricted to the United States, and peculiar in the sense of being strange or odd.

Important though the public statements of professional bodies may be, the abiding challenge is to produce better explanations. Chapters 4 and 5 discuss the ways in which sociologists have struggled with the use of race in ordinary language to structure social relations, and with the claim that a concept of racism might facilitate better explanations. Because of the country's history, the word 'race' in US English is loaded with a huge burden of varied meanings. It signifies much more than the same word does in UK English or in the corresponding words used in other European languages. Many sociologists, like those who prepared the 2002 ASA statement, have employed the ordinary language word instead of concluding that, for social science purposes, it needs to be replaced by a family of concepts that identify more accurately its analytically important components.

These doubts about the sociological value of the ordinary language notion of race reappear in the queries about the sociological value of ordinary language conceptions of ethnicity. These are rehearsed in chapter 6. Major problems remain that academics cannot solve by simply thinking harder, or by reanalysing existing knowledge. New research is needed, of a kind informed by a better understanding of the philosophical issues. Some possibilities are therefore discussed in chapter 7, leading through to the conclusion.

Notes

1. Retrieved 8 November 2012 from http://www.asanet.org/footnotes/september
toct02/indextwo.html.
2. AAPA Statement on Biological Aspects of Race, point 10. Retrieved 13 August 2012 from http://physanth.org/association/position-statemenrs/biological-aspects-of-race?searchterm=race.
3. Proposition 54 in the California ballot of 2003.
4. Kenneth Prewitt, *What is Your Race? The Census and Our Flawed Attempts to Classify Americans* (Princeton: Princeton University Press, 2013), 135.
5. Emile Durkheim, *Suicide: A Study in Sociology*, English translation edited by George Simpson (London: Routledge & Kegan Paul, 1952 [1897]). Henry Morselli, *Suicide: An Essay on Comparative Moral Statistics*, English translation (London: Kegan Paul, 1881). Barclay Johnson, 'Durkheim's One Cause of Suicide', *American Sociological Review* 1965 30(6): 875–886. Integration has been a central concept in recent discussions of the reception of migrants in European countries, but as yet sociologists have been unable to find any sociological concept that advances beyond Durkheim's conception of integration. Some students of migration write about 'migrant integration' as if the social integration of migrants differs from the integration of everyone else.

6. Max Weber also drew a distinction in kind between two vocabularies. He maintained that in contrast to historical writing (which must use constructs with multiple meanings), sociology must seek univocal constructs, each with but one meaning, and be *eindeutig*. See *Wirtschaft und Gesellschaft. Grundriss der Verstehenden Soziologie*, 5th edition (Tübingen: Mohr Siebeck, 1972), 9–10. Insofar as the difference between the two kinds of vocabulary poses a problem, the simple solution is to recognize the two forms of knowledge. Weber offered a more complex solution. It was in order to achieve *Eindeutigkeit* that he advocated the development of 'ideal types'. Many contemporary sociologists would recognize his ideal types as models. The full significance of Weber's distinction is not brought out in the *Economy and Society* translation of Weber's book.

7. James W. Lett, 'Emic/Etic Distinctions', in David Levinson and Melvin Ember (eds.), *Encyclopedia of Cultural Anthropology*, vol. 2 (New York: Holt, 1996), 382–383. Alternatively, see http://faculty.ircc.edu/faculty/jlett/.

8. Jennifer L. Hochschild, Vesla Weaver and Traci Burch, *Creating a New Racial Order: How Immigration, Multiracialism, Genomics, and the Young Can Remake Race in America* (Princeton: Princeton University Press, 2012).

1

The Scientific Sources
of the Paradox

The paradox at the heart of the ASA statement centred on the meanings given to 'race', a word that has been used in West European languages from the fifteenth century; first in Spanish from 1435, then in French from much the same time as in English, where it was recorded from the beginning of the sixteenth century. Over the centuries it has acquired additional meanings.

Two Dimensions

From the sixteenth to the eighteenth centuries the English people's ideas about themselves and about other peoples were structured by the anthropology of the Bible. This encouraged the belief that all humans descended from Adam, and that differences between them were to be explained genealogically. Whereas scholars wrote in Latin, 'race' entered as a word in the vernacular languages. From the beginning it had two dimensions of meaning. Its vertical dimension identified the historical origins of what made a set of persons distinctive, emphasizing heredity and genealogy. This meaning fitted with the anthropology of the Bible. It was exemplified in John Foxe's *Book of Martyrs*, of 1570, when he referred to 'the outward race and stocke of Abraham'. The word's horizontal dimension identified the nature of that distinctiveness.[1] There was no word in Latin that combined the two meanings of the word.

From the fifteenth to the eighteenth centuries the meaning given to the word primarily reflected the word's vertical dimension, identifying a set of persons sharing a common ancestry. This is the sense of race as lineage that is still sometimes evoked in the twenty-first century. While the two dimensions have always been present, over the past two centuries the horizontal dimension of meaning has often outweighed the vertical one.

Scholarly use of the word was sometimes influenced by popular thought. Some writers have therefore wondered whether use of the word 'race' indicated the presence of a racial consciousness. They have noted that in the sixteenth century writers in France started to interpret the history of their country as stemming from a clash between the indigenous Gauls and the invading Franks, and that the two were seen as distinct races. In England during the same century, defenders of the parliamentary cause against royal claims to rule by the 'divine right' turned to Tacitus's account of the customs of the Germans. They used this to maintain that the English were 'descended of German race' and that therefore the institution of monarchy was alien to them. Political clashes made religious differences important because the Catholic Church contended that the powers of the state should be used to support its faith.

Popular usage, however, has often been very loose, as can be illustrated by dictionary examples, such as John Milton's reference in *Paradise Lost* (1667) to 'the race of Satan'; by Sir Philip Sidney's approval (1580) of 'the race of good men'; and by Charles Lamb's 1821 essay on 'the two races of men' (who turn out to be 'the men who borrow and the men who lend'). Charles Kingsley, a Victorian cleric who had much to say about race, sometimes used the word very loosely, as when stating that 'there is no more beautiful race in Europe than the wives and daughters of our London shopkeepers'; when he lectured in Cambridge this terminological extravagance seems to have spread to his students, one of whom explained, 'for undergraduates are an affectionate race'.[2] Sir Winston Churchill wrote about the British as 'an island race', while in 1986 the House of Bishops of the General Synod of the Church of England declared that 'Jesus is also the "Second Adam", the Head of a new race in the Spirit'.

From the Renaissance until far into the eighteenth century most of the knowledge about human variation was synthesized in what was called natural theology.[3] Nature was to be studied as providing evidence for the belief in the Bible's record of creation and for a better understanding of the creator's plan. Thus a book by the pioneering biologist John Ray, published in 1691 and titled *The Wisdom of God Manifested in the Works of the Creation*, was described by Ernst Mayr as 'not only a powerful argument from design but also very sound natural history, indeed, one might say one of the earliest works of ecology'.[3] In this intellectual atmosphere little is to be gained from trying to separate the embryonic scientific knowledge from popular or practical knowledge.

Taxonomy

Such a separation becomes more useful with the publication in 1735 of Carl Linnaeus's great work that, over the next fifty-eight years, ran through thirteen editions. The tenth edition, which is considered the most important, bore the title *Systema naturæ, sive regna tria naturæ systematice proposita per classes, ordines, genera, & species* (translated as System of nature through the three kingdoms of nature, according to classes, orders, genera and species, with characters, differences, synonyms, places). The three kingdoms were the animal, vegetable and mineral. Over twelve thousand species of plants and animals were assigned to the categories of genus, species and varietas. The members of such categories are now called taxa and the name subspecies has superseded varietas.

By systematizing existing knowledge, Linnaeus offered a new understanding of the natural world, one that rested on the validity of the categories it employed. By 1766 the evidence of diversity within species was leading Linnaeus to entertain doubts about his assumption that God had created each species separately, and that no new species could arise. In the eighteenth century, these were fundamental issues. Other doubters at this time went further, one of them insisting, 'There are only individuals, and no kingdoms or classes or genera or species.'

The word 'race' did not feature in the Linnaean scheme, and had scholars continued to write in Latin and kept to his taxa, the ambiguity of the vernacular word might not have caused trouble. However, German scholars began to write of *rasse* and French scholars to write of *race* (in the French); they tried to insert this postulated category into the classification of genus, species and varietas without securing any agreement about how it related to the existing taxa. Thus in his magisterial work *Le Règne animal*, of 1817, Georges Cuvier (later Baron Cuvier) used the ordinary language word 'race' as a synonym for variety, stressing the horizontal dimension.

This is the true beginning of the history of race as a possible scientific concept. It is from this time onwards that the practical and theoretical forms of knowledge about biological inheritance can be distinguished.

Those who translated Cuvier's work into English faced a problem. His first English translator took it upon himself to reduce some of the confusion, for in the 1827 London translation, Cuvier's reference to 'certaines conformations héréditaires que constituent ce qu'on nomme des races' appears as 'which constitute what are called varieties'. Yet in the next English translation (published in New York in 1831) the sentence runs 'which constitute what are termed races', and 'race' is used thereafter.

Typology

The main source of scholarly debate about race in the nineteenth century was whether race could be equated with species or with subspecies. It was confounded by references to racial type. A new wave of writers, the racial typologists, stressed the horizontal dimension, the fact (for so they regarded it) that the main human stocks had always been distinct. That Europeans had developed further in technology and economic and political power was not in doubt. The question was whether the difference was attributable to circumstance, such as the nature of the environment, or, as the typologists maintained, that it was original and permanent. The word 'race' could be used in both kinds of explanation.

In the United States, Samuel Stanhope Smith, president of what was to become Princeton University, asserted in 1787 that Christians were not at liberty to question the Biblical account of creation. He maintained that the Negro form was changing so as to resemble the higher form of the whites. In a new and better environment, any inferiority would be overcome. Contemporaries who found explanations in biological inheritance were put on the defensive.

The main challenge to biblical orthodoxy came in 1839 when a Philadelphia doctor, Samuel George Morton, published *Crania Americana*; he reported his measurements of the internal capacity of a collection of skulls, and concluded that whites had the biggest brains, blacks the smallest and that browns came somewhere in between. This book, together with the more popular volumes by Josiah C. Nott and George R. Gilddon (notably *Types of Mankind* of 1854), constituted the American component of a new international school of thought. It maintained that distinctive racial types had existed throughout recorded history, each of which was suited to a particular continent or zoological province, and that individuals belonging to a particular racial type displayed an innate antagonism towards individuals belonging to other types.[4]

The French component of this school is best known through Arthur de Gobineau's four-volume essay, *The Inequality of Human Races* (1853–55). In Britain, the pioneer of racial typology was Charles Hamilton Smith, author of *The Natural History of the Human Species* (1848), but its first active propagandist was the Scottish anatomist, Robert Knox, author of *The Races of Man* (1850). In Germany, Karl Vogt published similar views.[5]

Some typologists held that pure races had existed in the past, and that, because their distinctiveness was related to natural environments, they would eventually repurify themselves. Others, like Gobineau, held that the mixing had gone too far and that the process of decline could not be halted. Their theories were pre-Darwinian attempts to account for human diversity and were often vehicles for the political opinions of their exponents. If humans belonged in races, was this classification to be equated with the distinctiveness of a species or a variety? For blacks and whites to be accounted separate species, it would have been necessary to establish that hybrids between them were infertile. This was obviously not the case, so the typologists were stymied. The confusion was such that in 1863 the president of the Anthropological Society of London complained that 'science can make no advance while hardly two persons use such an important word as race in the same sense'.

By this time the word 'race' had nevertheless gained a secure place in the ordinary language of English speakers. It was so effective in organizing much existing information about humans, including popular conceptions of their history on the earth, that many of those interested in human differences assumed that it must be a taxonomic category of some sort. The next chapter will trace the process by which the typological conception became so important in popular thought in the United States. This chapter will remark on how in the twenty-first century it could still influence the interpretation of new scientific findings.

Darwin and Mendel

In the 1830s Darwin thought of species as forms that were kept distinct by reproductive isolation. He wondered how it was that plants apparently belonging to the same species could be found on widely separated islands in the Pacific. Could their seeds have floated on ocean currents? So he investigated wind speeds and conducted experiments to see how long such seeds could survive in salt water. In this way he could reach an explanation of an observation. Why did the peacock have so big a tail when it impeded flight and might attract predators? Darwin's answer was that the females of the species inherited a preference for mating with the males who could make the finest display; it was his theory of sexual selection. In each case an observation identified a problem within the existing framework of knowledge, and, by the discovery of an explanation, knowledge grew.

By 1859 Darwin had come to believe that the term 'species' was 'one arbitrarily given for the sake of convenience to a set of individuals closely resembling each other, and that it does not essentially differ from the term variety'.[6] The Linnaean distinctions of 1758 did not help him find explanations of the things that puzzled him. In their endeavours to see if species and varieties could be separated, botanists made more rapid progress than zoologists because plants could be bred in cultivation more quickly than animals (though of course Darwin took an intense interest in the breeding of pigeons). The botanists could more easily identify the contributions of particular chromosomes than their colleagues in other fields.

Darwin did not use the word race with the meaning that became dominant in the twentieth-century USA. His focus was always on the explanation of differences and similarities. Classification was important in so far as it aided explanation; it was not an end in itself. Noting the lack of agreement about taxonomic criteria in twelve notable classifications of human races, Darwin observed that 'the most weighty of all the arguments against treating the races of man as distinct species is that they graduate into each other, independently ... of their having intercrossed'. Every naturalist confronted with such a problem, he wrote, 'will end by uniting all the forms which graduate into each other as a single species; for he will say to himself that he has no right to give names to objects which he cannot define'. Already by 1871 Darwin recognized the power of the ordinary language construct of race when, having noted that the human forms in question might appropriately be called sub-species, he concluded, perhaps sadly, that 'from long habit the term "race" will perhaps always be employed'. Returning to his main point, he stated that 'it is almost a matter of indifference whether the so-called races of man... are ranked as species or sub-species'[7]. His profession of indifference on a matter many considered vital should make every reader pause.

It looks as if Darwin professed indifference because his concern was with variation. That was his explanandum, the set of facts to be accounted for. The typological concept of race had been advanced as part of an argument about whether different varieties of Homo sapiens had a common progenitor. Darwin preferred not to be involved in this argument. He was far from indifferent about research into what in ordinary language were called 'domestic races' (like pigeons and dogs) because the study of breeding practices could offer clues to the sources of biological variation. If, from 'long habit' (i.e., in ordinary language), people regarded racial differences as facts they were building ideas of race into their explanandum, assuming it had explanatory value, instead of seeing whether it was useful as part of an explanans.

Though Darwin's discoveries destroyed any notion of permanent racial types, this was not immediately apparent. The scientific implications of the theory of natural selection were complex, and became more so with the belated discovery in 1900 of the results of Gregor Mendel's experiments with peas, for they helped explain what determined the inheritance of their characters. A fierce dispute followed between the biometricians, who took their lead from Francis Galton's law of ancestral heredity, and the Mendelians. The former focussed on continuous variation as analysed by Darwin, the latter on the discontinuous variation that sprang from mutation. On a strict interpretation of the growth of knowledge, the history of race as a candidate for entry into the vocabulary of science came to an end once the significance of Mendel's discoveries was appreciated. The place it sought went instead to the concept of phenotype, defined by Wilhelm Johannsen in 1909 as 'the sum total of the observable features of an individual, regarded as the consequence of the interaction of its genotype with its environment'.[8] Johannsen was the Danish botanist who coined the word 'gene' for the unit of inheritance.

The process of eliminating race as a possible scientific concept was completed when, in the 1920s, the mathematician R. A. Fisher subsumed the biometricians' and the Mendelians' explanations in a new model of the processes of inheritance. His 1930 book, *The Genetical Theory of Natural Selection*, showed, among much else, that it was the gene, and not the species, that was the unit of selection. Together with the biochemist J. B. S. Haldane and the US geneticist Sewell Wright, he helped create the new field of population genetics.[9]

Seen in retrospect, it looks as if the Darwinian revolution of 1859 took some seventy years to complete and that it was a prelude to further revolutions in biology highlighted by Francis Crick and James Watson's discovery of the structure of the DNA molecule in 1953, and Craig Venter's sequencing of the entire human genome in 2000. A point to note, however, is that it took a generation for some anthropologists to appreciate the significance of population genetics for the study of 'racial' variation. In the meantime, popular ideas about race had done great damage. Opinion in the wider public was engaged by a movement, sometimes called Social Darwinism, in which some authors advanced a selectionist theory according to which, possibly aided by eugenicist measures, selection would create pure races in the future.

Two Vocabularies

The first lesson that the sociologist of race relations can draw from this history is that, within a little less than a hundred years, the ordinary language conception of race as a division, of either the Hominidae or of *Homo sapiens,* could gain such a hold in the minds of Europeans and North Americans that even the specialists had difficulty liberating their work from it. After an interval, it is now possible to trace the course by which knowledge grew. Moreover, hindsight makes it possible to see that the contrast between a social conception of race and a supposed biological concept only confers respectability upon an idea that was never properly accepted in biological science. The popular impression of race as a biological concept lingered because the eugenics movement captured public attention and because – in a diffuse fashion – it attracted politically motivated support. Most of the anthropologists of this generation could not cope with the reorientation demanded by new biological knowledge. Their disorientation was demonstrated by the failure of the 1934 'Race and Culture' committee of the Royal Anthropological Institute in London to agree on which forms of human variation could be explained as the outcome of biological inheritance.[10]

The second lesson is that, by seeking explanations of puzzling observations, knowledge about human variation never ceases to grow. The sociologist gains little from trying to ascertain the very most up-to-date account of thought in genetics because knowledge in this field is growing so rapidly that any statement may quickly be rendered out of date by the publication of new findings. In no scientific field can knowledge be regarded as static. In the social sciences, the growth of knowledge follows the same rules, though it has to grow within a more contentious political environment, both international and national.

This summary account of the scientific sources of the 2002 paradox can continue by noting that one of the earliest actions of the United Nations was to ask UNESCO (the United Nations Educational, Scientific and Cultural Organization) to initiate and recommend 'the general adoption of a programme of disseminating scientific facts designed to remove what is commonly known as racial prejudice'. Setting about its task, UNESCO consulted a variety of experts. It was striking to note that in the 1950s some experts in physical anthropology still had not properly assimilated the implications of population genetics for their conceptions of race. The geneticists were starting from observations that bore upon hypotheses and were challenging the concepts used in their field; the errant anthropologists, on the other hand, were assuming that race was an appropriate concept for the purposes in question. They were forcing new observations into an obsolete framework.[11] In any field of inquiry there can be a problem of how to identify and dispose of scientific waste.

Correspondence in *Current Anthropology* in the mid-1960s showed the continuing strength of comparative morphology in Poland. In Vienna prior to 1993, the Natural History Museum included a hall known as the *Rassensaal*; this displayed a series of exhibits representing the 'human family' as divided into three 'great races' and a series of types. Though from a scientific point of view the display was at least twenty years out of date, it needed a public controversy to elicit a promise of modernization.[12]

In 1978 the General Conference of UNESCO, consisting of representatives of all member states, adopted by acclamation a Declaration on Race and Racial Prejudice. In Article 1 it proclaimed, 'All human beings belong to a single species.' This statement came a century late, for by 1978 knowledge had moved on, and species membership was no longer a critical issue in biological science. Other concepts were more important to scientific progress.

The story of what happened to the proposed concept of race in the nineteenth century illustrates the nature of theoretical concepts (as opposed to the conceptions of ordinary language) that was mentioned in the introduction. In the contexts in which ordinary language is used, fine distinctions or possible ambiguities may not be important. Ordinary language words often acquire new meanings. Thus the 2002 ASA description of race as 'a principal category in the organization of daily social life' called up associations with the black-white divide and relied upon a meaning that the word did not have a century earlier.

Technical language seeks, among alternative definitions, a single, agreed definition; the one with the greatest explanatory power is preferred. This is an external criterion of selection. Mendel isolated the paired units of heredity, now known as genes, as occurring in alternative forms: AA and aa in the parental varieties, and Aa in the hybrids. Mendel called the character that prevailed in the hybrid dominant, and the one that appeared to be suppressed recessive. These were two new technical, or etic, constructs. The point to note is that the constructs were the outcome of the experiments that made their creation necessary. New discoveries necessitated the coining of new words.

The distinction between the two kinds of knowledge is conceptual, and it can be difficult to trace because some words that have single meanings in a theoretical language may also be used much less precisely in popular speech (e.g. 'mass', 'force' and 'momentum' have technical meanings in physics but are also used in ordinary language). The value of the distinction is exemplified by words (like 'angels' and 'witches') that have no corresponding realities. Some savants thought there was a field of study known as alchemy, full of words that proved to be without corresponding things. Within science, there have been concepts like phlogiston that proved to be similarly empty and had to be expelled from the technical vocabulary. Just as there may be no reality corresponding to 'species', so, as will be argued later, there may be no realities corresponding to the words 'race' and 'ethnicity'.

The concept of species is a further example of the difficulties that arise because, quite apart from its use in ordinary language, there is not yet any agreement on its best use in the technical language of biology. Ernst Mayr found it vital to distinguish an essentialist conception of species from a nominalist one.[13] He updated an older distinction between realist and nominalist definitions. An essentialist (or realist) definition seeks to grasp the most essential quality of the thing in question. A nominalist definition seeks to distinguish the thing from other things with which it might be confused. A favourite example is Aristotle's realist definition of the human being as a rational animal, compared with the nominalist definition of that creature as a featherless biped. For some purposes, particularly in ordinary language, a realist definition may do what is required. For other purposes, particularly in scientific inquiry, only a nominalist definition will be fit for purpose.

Karl Popper, who introduced the notion of essentialism, wrote:

> I use the name methodological essentialism to characterize the view, held by Plato and many of his followers, that it is the task of pure knowledge or 'science' to discover and describe the true nature of things, i.e., their hidden reality or essence. It was Plato's peculiar belief that the essence of sensible things can be found in other and more real things – in their primogenitors or Forms.[14]

So Plato did not problematize the relation between the thing and the word. He thought of 'forms' as things difficult to grasp. According to Popper, that relation was better addressed by methodological nominalism, an approach that searches for whatever words best describe how a thing behaves in various circumstances and studies any regularities in its behaviour.

This argument harks back to a famous passage in Immanuel Kant's *Critique of Pure Reason*:

> Hitherto it has been assumed that all our knowledge must conform to objects. But all attempts to extend our knowledge of objects by establishing something in regard to them a priori, by means of concepts, have, on this assumption, ended in failure. We must therefore make trial whether we may not have more success in the tasks of metaphysics, if we suppose that objects must conform to our knowledge.

This was the basis of Kant's 'Copernican revolution' in the study of knowledge.[15]

The revolution can be exemplified by an analogy with the use of a grid in the construction and interpretation of maps. Coordinates are imposed on the map like a net, and the location of any point can be determined by reading off the numbers on two dimensions. Concepts are like that net. They justify their existence by the part they play in explanation. While they may also feature in ordinary language, the words that make up technical languages are subject to challenge as the growth of knowledge leads to better explanations.

The discovery that it was the gene, and not the species, that was the unit of selection forced major changes in the theoretical grid. It superseded any argument for race as a taxonomic category in the most effective of all ways, by opening the way to better explanations of biological differences. Such a path was outlined in a much-quoted article of Richard Lewontin in 1972.[16] On the basis of his research, he reported that most of the variation (80–85 per cent) within human populations is found within local geographic groups and that differences attributable to so-called races are a minor part of human genetic variability (1–15 per cent). This finding does not always bear the construction that has been put upon it.[17] There is now general agreement that if a great number of genetic characters are examined, statistical associations will be found to show inherited similarities shared by individuals who have a common ethnic origin, but only in very special circumstances, such as in planning the provision of medical services, are these associations of social significance.

The new knowledge contributed by research in genetics could be used, either to challenge, and possibly change, the US ordinary language conception of race, or to reinforce the original error embodied in the one-drop rule.

The Power of the Ordinary Language Construct

Eventually the US ordinary language conception of phenotypical categories will be brought into line with new scientific knowledge, but it will not easily be done because the popular conception is reinforced so strongly in daily life. A New York professor reported in 2011 that she had been required to report her race when submitting school applications, renting an apartment, getting a marriage certificate, applying for work as a college professor, being fingerprinted for government job clearance, obtaining research funding and filling out the household census form.[18] The forms that have to be completed rarely provide any definition of 'race' or state the purpose for which this information is required. In the United States, therefore, one source of the ordinary language construct's power is inertia. Once a classificatory procedure like this has been embedded in social institutions, an equal force has to be mobilized if it is to be changed.

When the same procedure is used for so many different purposes, confusion is inevitable. Some sort of classification is needed if patients are to be screened for inherited diseases, such as sickle-cell anaemia, cystic fibrosis, Down syndrome and Tay-Sachs disease among Ashkenazi Jews. In 2001, because of their concern about such conditions, the American Colleges of Obstetricians and Gynaecologists and of Medical Genetics issued guidelines recommending that cystic fibrosis carrier screening be offered to Caucasian couples, including Ashkenazi Jews, if they were planning a pregnancy or seeking prenatal care.[19] Such couples may well be identified in a medical setting and be interviewed by someone using guidelines that specify the social categories to be used. More serious problems arise with self-completion forms because any options they offer need to use categories familiar to those who are asked to fill in the forms.[20] Public controversies, like the one that led to the 2002 ASA statement, could be used to call more loudly for the updating of such modes of data collection. This would need to be based upon close consultation with data users and with those who design forms and classify responses. If the revised forms avoided use of the word 'race' and referred, as some official forms already do, to 'subgroups of the population', these new alternatives would weaken some sources of misunderstanding.

The ASA statement drew attention to differences in life expectancy, mortality and the incidence of certain health conditions (for example, African Americans had higher death rates than whites for eight of the ten leading causes of death). Access to affordable medical care also varied, as did the salubrity of residential neighbourhoods. The statement did not comment upon possible inherited susceptibilities to particular diseases.

Two years earlier, at a White House ceremony to publicize the significance of the completion of the first draft of the human genome, President Clinton had declared that 'in genetic terms, all human beings, regardless of race, are more than 99.9 per cent the same'. Craig Venter had followed with the statement that 'the concept of race has no genetic or scientific basis'. Since then, though knowledge about the genetic transmission of health conditions has been growing at an unprecedented rate, some of those involved have been slow to learn all the lessons it teaches.

Nothing illustrates the restraining power of the ordinary language construct better than the grounds on which, in 2005, the US Food and Drug Administration (FDA) 'approved BiDil, a drug for the treatment of heart failure in self-identified black patients, representing a step towards the promise of personalized medicine'.[21] The chair of the panel stated, 'We are using self-identified race as a surrogate for genomic-based medicine.'[22] As the critics pointed out, 'self-identified black patients' would include many persons with more European than African ancestry. 'Personalized medicine' could not be based on self-identifications but would have to be based on each individual's actual genome. Some commentators deplored the licensing of the drug for a socially, not medically, defined section of the population, seeing it as a revival of 'race-based medicine' or 'racialized medicine'.[23]

Variations in susceptibility to particular health conditions, like heart disease, constitute an explanandum. While it is conceivable that race, in some sense of that troublesome word, might constitute part of an explanans, some researchers have built their own conception of race into their explanandum. A leading expert on the genetics of asthma has collected thousands of genetic samples, stored by race in the his university's DNA bank, to create a database his lab team can scan for genetic clues as to what distinguishes rates of asthma in different racial and ethnic groups.

His database consisted of 24 African American, 96 Puerto Rican, 96 Mexican, 86 Caucasian and 7 Asian asthmatics. A comparison of their genomes claimed to have uncovered a relevant mutation specific 'to African origin'. The hypothesis that the condition is caused by the mutation was checked against other possible causes, while the claim that the sample was adequate to sustain a generalization about 'African origin' must be questioned.[24] That these and other considerations can be passed over shows how the strength of the ordinary language construct can feature in the explanandum. It does not belong there.

That construct is also built into some of the commentary on the BiDil episode. The author of a very well-documented and reasoned examination of how the FDA handled the application from a pharmaceutical company, and the possible influence of commercial interests, continually refers to the 'race-specific' presentation of this and other drugs. He gave his book the catchy title *Race in a Bottle*,[25] the choice of which should recall a sentence in the statement of the American Association of Physical Anthropologists that was quoted earlier. The tense in that quotation could equally well have read that 'there never has been any national, religious, linguistic or cultural group or economic class that constituted a race'. If that view of the history of science is accepted, there can be no justification for an expression like 'race-specific' or for use of the word 'race' in a book's title. What may have appeared to be 'race' in the bottle was put there because in the United States use of the ordinary language construct in an inappropriate context occasions only feeble objection. It ignores the damage done by the recycling of a pernicious error.

The passions of the genomicists whose research has made possible the growth in knowledge about the genetics of disease figure in Catherine Bliss's book, *Race Decoded: The Genomic Fight for Social Justice*.[26] The reader should pause over this title also. Why does it refer to the decoding of race rather than the decoding of biological diversity or of human variability?[27] The author's account of her interviews suggests that the genomicists see genetic differences as their explananda. They are bitterly critical of the requirements for federal funding that require them to employ the census categories dictated by the Office of Management and Budget. The same passages also suggest that genomicists are just as much, or even more, aware of the political issues as some of the critics who express alarm about possible misconceptions and misrepresentations. The causes for concern arise most strongly in connection with the processes for granting patents to the manufacturers of pharmaceuticals and with the language manufacturers use in the pursuit of their commercial interests. It is the federal government that is primarily responsible for the misconceptions and misrepresentations, although some journalists have added to misunderstanding by oversimplifying the issues.

One concern underlying criticism of some of the current vocabulary of genomics is the possible effect that some FDA approvals and other apparently authoritative pronouncements have upon popular sentiment. To achieve a social reform in an industrialized society it is usually necessary to mobilize collective action. The effectiveness of pressure groups depends upon the readiness of potential activists to identify with a cause, and in recent times 'identity politics' have offered their supporters a means to the exercise of influence. Campaigning requires the use of ordinary language and emic constructs; the vocabulary introduced with what are sometimes called 'the new genetics' has been pictured as a tactic used to undermine identity politics.[28]

An important article contributed to a symposium in a leading genetics journal acknowledged 'the potential for furthering racism by discussing race and genetics together', but concluded, 'Given current health disparities, however, and assuming that our society values the goal of understanding the underlying basis of those disparities, the continued use of labels in epidemiological research and clinical practice seems justified.'[29]

Ann Morning has published the findings of her research into the question, 'How do scientists think and teach about human differences?' The report on her research illustrates the influence of the emic construct of race upon the mindset of the author as well as upon many of her interviewees. It shows what happens when an inquiry starts from a word instead of from an intellectual problem (in this case, that of how best to account for human differences). She asked anthropologists and biologists whether they agreed or disagreed with the statement 'there are biological races in the species *Homo sapiens*'. That there is phenotypical variation within the species *Homo sapiens* is incontestable. Whether the word 'race' serves to identify that variation is the critical issue, but that issue was excluded from consideration. The anthropologists who were interviewed said that they discussed race in many contexts, some of them in connection with physical differences, some in connection with cultural or historical questions. Biologists, however, were evenly divided over whether it came within their scope.[30] It may be that some biologists introduced mention of race in order to contribute to their students' general education rather than because they could not explain the biology without it.

Everything turns on the purpose for which the word is employed. Is it used in an ordinary language sense simply as a 'label' that designates a set of individuals, or is it a concept essential to the explanation of a theoretical puzzle? John Stuart Mill regarded the distinction between terms that only denote and concepts that connote as one of the most important distinctions in logic, and as one of those distinctions 'which go deepest into the nature of language'. He wrote that 'a non-connotative term is one which signifies a subject only, or an attribute only. A connotative term is one which denotes a subject and implies an attribute.'[31]

If the definition of *Homo sapiens* as a featherless biped is an example of a nominalist definition, it locates the subject in the biped category and differentiates it from other members of that category. A label is a poor relation of such a definition because it simply identifies something without necessarily placing it in any class. It does not connote anything, and its use should not be an occasion for concern.

As this chapter has demonstrated, race may be used in either an emic or an etic sense. Foxe's reference to 'the outward race and stocke of Abraham' was an emic usage that denoted the descendants of Abraham. If it was used to explain the plan on which God assembled his Creation, it was connotative and might therefore be a concept in the full sense of that word. In contemporary circumstances, race may be used as a label to designate a line of individuals who have inherited a specific genetic characteristic, like sickle-cell anaemia, cystic fibrosis, Tay-Sachs or haemophilia, simply because no better designation is at hand. This is the sense in which the word most often appears in the writing of Darwin and many of the next generation of biologists; it exemplifies the word's vertical dimension as opposed to the horizontal dimension employed in the racial classifications of the late nineteenth and early twentieth centuries.[32] These classifications claimed explanatory value, as accounting for the history and character of a category of persons.

The distinction between two kinds of knowledge enables the reader to conclude that while race has a prominent place in the ordinary language vocabulary, it has none in the vocabulary of science. It appears nowhere in Mayr's very substantial account of the growth of biological thought. Nor does it feature in the *International Code of Zoological Nomenclature*. It is not an explanatory concept in biology, and the American Association of Physical Anthropologists issued their statement about the biological aspects of race only because the word had gained such an important place in the ordinary language vocabulary.

Sociologists can learn lessons from the history summarized in this chapter. Many discussions of the history of racial thought start from the use that has been made of the word, treating all uses as equally legitimate. This chapter has argued that it is more informative to start from a consideration of the purpose for which the word has been employed in order to examine how well it serves a purpose. It has stressed the importance of accurately identifying a problem that calls for explanation.

Sociologists can analyse the process by which the ordinary language conception has become so powerful in the United States, especially since 1865, surviving the challenges from technical language in 1909 (Johannsen), 1930 (Fisher) and 2000 (Venter). While they cannot undertake the sorts of experiments that Mendel conducted, a later chapter will contend that, like social psychologists, sociologists can design studies that will lead to observations of a standardized character, and then look to see what best accounts for their special features. They can concentrate upon the study of problems that are capable of explanation.

Notes

1. Michael Banton, 'The Vertical and Horizontal Dimensions of the Word Race', *Ethnicities* 2010 10(1): 127–140. Naomi Zack, *Philosophy of Science and Race* (New York: Routledge, 2002), 40–57, draws a distinction between vertical and horizontal models of human differences that in some respects parallels this distinction between ways in which the word 'race' has been used.

2. For Kingsley and early uses of the word in English, see Michael Banton, *The Idea of Race* (London: Tavistock, 1977).

3. Ernst Mayr, *The Growth of Biological Thought: Diversity, Evolution, and Inheritance* (Cambridge, MA: Harvard University Press, 1982), 104.

4. For the typological school, see Michael Banton, *Racial Theories*, 2nd edition (Cambridge: Cambridge University Press, 1997). For examples of the diversity in the attempts between 1864 and 1880 to give the word theoretical significance, see Michael D. Biddiss (ed.), *Images of Race* (Leicester: Leicester University Press, 1979).

5. Those who wrote about race in the mid- and late nineteenth century are sometimes described as 'race scientists'. Prichard, Morton, Nott, Smith, Knox and Vogt were medical doctors; Gliddon and Gobineau had no academic qualifications. Apart from Cuvier, few were engaged full-time in anything resembling science as this word is understood in the twenty-first century, so this and similar expressions, such as 'scientific racism', can convey a misleading impression.

6. Mayr, *The Growth of Biological Thought*, 267.

7. Quotations from Chapter VII of *The Descent of Man, and Selection in Relation to Sex*, 1871, forming part of Edward O. Wilson, ed., *From So Simple A Beginning. The Four Great Books of Charles Darwin* (New York: Norton, 2006), pp. 905–910. Amidst the impressive literature on Darwin's reasoning, a special place should be reserved for a book by a great-great-grandson of his, Randal Keynes, *Annie's Box. Charles Darwin, his Daughter and Human Evolution* (London: Fourth Estate, 2001).

8. Wilhelm Johannsen, *Elemente der Exakten Erblichkeitslehre* (Jena: Gustav Fischer, 1909).

9. William B. Provine, *The Origins of Theoretical Population Genetics* (Chicago: University of Chicago Press, 1971). For informative accounts of the personalities of R. A. Fisher, J. B. S. Haldane, and some other leading biologists, see Marek Kohn, *A Reason for Everything: Natural Selection and the English Imagination* (London: Faber, 2004).

10. Elazar Barkan, *The Retreat of Scientific Racism: Changing concepts of race in Britain and the United States between two world wars* (Cambridge: Cambridge University Press, 1992), pp. 285–296. Barkan's book offers an admirable account of its subject matter, a series of failed explanantia. In contrast, the present book attempts to start from the social significance of phenotypical characteristics as an explanandum.

11. UNESCO, T*he Race Concept* (Paris: UNESCO, 1953), pp. 34–65. Also, Michael Banton, *The International Politics of Race* (Cambridge: Polity, 2002), pp. 28–38.

12. Marek Kohn, *The Race Gallery. The Return of Racial Science* (London: Cape, 1995).
13. Mayr, op.cit. pp. 256–265.
14. Karl R. Popper, *The Poverty of Historicism* (London: Routledge, 1957), pp. 26–34.
15. For an earlier discussion, see Michael Banton, 'Epistemological Assumptions in the Study of Racial Differentiation' in John Rex and David Mason, editors, *Theories of Race and Ethnic Relations* (Cambridge: Cambridge University Press, 1986), pp. 42–63.
16. Richard Lewontin, 'The Apportionment of Human Diversity', *Evolutionary Biology* 1972 6: 391–398.
17. The importance of genetical differences within as well as between continental populations is highlighted in Nicholas Wade, *A Troublesome Inheritance: Genes, Race. Genes, Race and Human History*, 2014 New York: Penguin. He writes of 'the fact of race' as if the popular US conception were the explanandum. Had he separated practical and theoretical knowledge, his case would have been stronger.
18. Ann Morning, *The Nature of Race: How Scientists Think and Teach About Human Difference* (Berkeley: University of California Press, 2011), p. 2.
19. For speculations about the possible causes of Jewish success in certain fields, and of Jewish susceptibility to certain specific diseases, see Wade, op. cit., pp. 198–214.
20. Peter J. Aspinall, 'When is the Use of Race/Ethnicity Appropriate in Risk Assessment Tools for Preconceptual or Antenatal Genetic Screening and How should it be Used?' *Sociology*, 2013 47(5): 957–975.
21. Dorothy Roberts, *Fatal Invention: How Science, Politics and Big Business Re-Create Race in the Twenty-first Century* (New York: New Press, 2011), p. 165.
22. Jonathan Kahn, *Race in a Bottle: The Story of BiDil and Racialized Medicine in a Post-Genomic Age* (New York: Columbia University Press, 2012), p. 163.
23. On the use of 'racialization', see Karim Murji & John Solomos, eds., *Racialization: Studies in Theory and Practice* (Cambridge: Cambridge University Press, 2005), pp. 1–27, 51–68.
24. See Roberts, op. cit., pp. 109–111.
25. Kahn, ibid.
26. Catherine Bliss, *Race Decoded: The Genomic Fight for Social Justice* (Stanford: Stanford University Press, 2012)
27. 'The scientists I spoke with suggest that they are getting closer to a solution and thus require more investment in research that will shed light on the true nature of human variation'. This may be contrasted with the author's statement 'I view race as a belief system…' Ibid. pp. 11–12, 14. At the present time, *Race Decoded* is important reading for anyone interested in recent developments. Some of the references to 'race as ancestry' and to 'race as a stratifying practice' (p. 85) parallel what has been written above about the vertical and horizontal meanings given to the word.
28. Catherine Bliss, 'The Marketization of Identity Politics', *Sociology*, 2013 47(5): 1011–1; Katharina Schramm, David Skinner & Richard Rottenburg, eds., *Identity Politics and the New Genetics* (New York: Berghahn, 2012).

29. Joanna L. Mountain & Neil Risch, 'Assessing genetic contributions to phenotypic differences among 'racial' and 'ethnic' groups', *Nature Genetics* 2004 36(11) S48–53.

30. Ann Morning, op. cit., pp. 138–141. For an update, see her 'And you thought we had moved beyond all that', 2014 37(10): 1676–1685.

31. John Stuart Mill, *A System of Logic: Ratiocinative and Inductive* (London, originally 1843), Book 1, Chapter II, section 5.

32. See Provine, op. cit., pp. 131–132, and the reference to Mendel as starting with a population of peas 'formed by the hybridization of races AA and aa'; it is followed by the statistician G. Udney Yule's question about what happens if 'the two races A and a are left to themselves'. These are examples of the use of a name, race, simply to denote a subject and not to make any meaningful statement about how the subject fits into any explanatory scheme.

2

The Political Sources
of the Paradox

When Europeans, Africans and Amerindians met with one another in the New World, they differed in many ways, both physically and culturally (especially in language, religion and technical abilities). The Europeans expected an Indian to be of Indian appearance, of Indian ancestry and to lead a conventional Indian existence. An African was supposed to be of black appearance, of African ancestry, illiterate and a pagan. A European was expected to look like a European, to be of European descent, a Christian and to behave like a European.

The reality often failed to match these expectations. The practical difficulties in establishing viable settlements in a strange land made expediency more important than social distinctions. Several European powers struggled for new territory and entered into alliances with whoever could help them. Amerindians, Europeans and Africans mixed and mated. One leading historian has found that black life in mainland North America began in the seventeenth century with the Atlantic Creoles serving as intermediaries, employing their linguistic skills and their familiarity with the Atlantic's diverse commercial practices, cultural conventions and diplomatic etiquette to mediate between the merchants and the sea captains.[1]

The distinctiveness of Creoles as a social group was not to last, even if, for a time, French and Spanish influences gave a different character to black-white relations in Charleston, in Florida and in New Orleans. By the mid-eighteenth century, Britain had thirteen flourishing colonies on the Atlantic coast, several of them clustered around Chesapeake Bay. They declared their independence in 1776. Parts in the south of what were to become the United States were controlled by other European powers, sometimes changing hands between France and Spain, while a huge stretch of land west of the Mississippi became part of the United States by the Louisiana Purchase in 1803.

Social Categories and Their Names

The English settlers in North America were at first inclined to refer to themselves as Christians and to Africans as Negroes. In the beginning of the seventeenth century they began more frequently to call themselves 'English' and 'free', and then, after about 1680, to be 'white'. The author of a very substantial study of American attitudes towards the Negro between 1550 and 1812 refers at times to 'the races', but it is important to remember that during this period it was unusual for the people themselves to employ the idiom of race in ordinary speech or writing.[2]

In Britain, up to the end of the eighteenth century, a person's religious faith seems to have been regarded as the most important indicator of how he or she should be socially classified. Attending a particular church or chapel could serve as a sign of political alignment or social position, and seems usually to have outweighed any consideration of a person's skin colour. The signs of socio-economic position, such as costume, speech and manner, were more important than phenotype.[3] There were no racial categories.

The word 'race' made a prominent appearance in popular English-language literature with the publication in 1820 of Sir Walter Scott's enormously successful novel *Ivanhoe*. Describing life in an age that has been popularized by films about Robin Hood, Scott presented the struggle between the Norman conquerors of England and the indigenous Saxons as the struggle between two races. Often he referred to race in the sense of lineage, drawing on the vertical significance of the word, but on other occasions the difference between Saxons and Normans was presented as insuperable. This, and other historical romances, laid the basis for a popular conception of race as marking a fundamental difference between two peoples.

The writings of Thomas Jefferson, a contemporary of Scott's, have been said to constitute 'the most intense, extensive, and extreme formulation of anti-Negro "thought" offered by any American in the thirty years after the Revolution'.[4] In Jefferson's day, the word 'race' lacked any precise meaning. Confronted by three kinds of human, Jefferson turned three into two by transforming the Indian into a degraded but basically noble brand of white man; about 'the blacks whether originally a distinct race, or made distinct by time or circumstances', he was unsure. Yet even when defending slavery, Virginians seem to have felt no need to advance suggestions of permanent Negro inferiority. For many whites, the Bible furnished the best justifications for enslavement.

The effects of the plantation as a social form were extensive. It was with the conception of slavery as 'a positive good', proclaimed by John C. Calhoun in 1837, that the doctrine of permanent black inferiority began its career as a rationale, first for slavery itself and later for post-emancipation forms of racial oppression. In the era of slavery, the idiom of race (that is, the use of words like 'race' and 'racial') was employed in print by writers who set out to explain observed or alleged differences between the major human groups,[5] but in popular speech blacks were usually referred to as Negroes (without the capital letter), or as 'coloured', or as slaves.

In the 1857 Dred Scott decision, the US Supreme Court held that 'the legislation and histories of the times, and the language used in the Declaration of Independence, show, that neither the class of persons who had been imported as slaves, nor their descendants, whether they had become free or not, were then acknowledged as a part of the people, nor intended to be included in the general words used in that memorable instrument'. Though the Court referred to Dred Scott as 'a negro of the African race', it used race to denote a category of people. It denied Scott's appeal on the grounds of the enslavement of his ancestors. Its reference to 'the African race' may, for some people, have carried connotations of black inferiority, but the Court's judgment was based on constitutional reasoning.

After the ending of slavery and the passage of the Fifteenth Amendment to the US Constitution, white southerners no longer had use for Calhoun's arguments and could not rely on the reasoning of the Supreme Court. Yet they still needed a name for that category of persons who had previously been enslaved. Given all the difficulties posed for them by the presence of persons who looked as if they might have been enslaved, but were free, it suited their interests to highlight the black-white distinction by a greater use of the idiom of 'race'. Robert Park grasped only half the story when he wrote: 'Generally speaking, there was no such thing as a race problem before the Civil War and there was at that time very little of what we ordinarily call race prejudice, except in the case of the free Negro. The free Negro was the source and origin of whatever race problems there were.'[6]

Park's statement noted a major change in the language in which black-white relations were represented, even if his reference to 'race problems' read back into the pre-1865 period a conception of race problems that developed only later, while his use of the expression 'problem' was but a euphemism for a history of white brutality in behaviour towards 'the free Negro'.

In Charleston (South Carolina) and New Orleans (Louisiana) there were, for many decades, distinctive communities of people of partly African and partly European descent occupying positions intermediate between whites and slaves. In such places there might be a colour scale divided into three, with one line between whites and part-whites and another line dividing these two social categories from the blacks.[7] Whites wanted to classify members of the intermediate communities with those called 'the free Negros'. They constituted 'a problem' only in the eyes of those whites who wanted to enforce a colour line that subordinated all blacks to all whites. In the years preceding the Civil War, southern states enacted more and more laws to force free blacks into slavery.

How had Negro slavery come about in the first place? Winthrop Jordan concluded that 'there is simply not enough evidence (and very little chance of more to come) to show precisely when and how and why Negroes came to be treated so differently from white men'.[8] That they should be treated differently he called an 'unthinking decision'. After the Civil War there was another unthinking decision, one by which persons who had previously been known as 'free' and 'slave' were assigned together to a social category constructed as 'racial' instead of as one denoting skin colour. The power to name a social category can have massive political consequences, the greater if the chosen name comes to be unquestioned and no alternatives are canvassed. The white introduction of a 'racial' vocabulary in the United States is a case in point.

After the Civil War

The position of the United State's indigenous peoples had been established as quite different from that of blacks. The Supreme Court in its 1857 Dred Scott decision had spoken very respectfully of Indians, saying that 'although they were uncivilized, they were yet a free and independent people, associated together in nations or tribes, and governed by their own laws. … These Indian Governments were regarded and treated as foreign Governments, Treaties have been negotiated with them, and their alliance sought for in war.' Jefferson was not the only person engaged in turning three races into two.[9]

Both before and after the Civil War, there was widespread hostility towards the Negro cause in the northern states, motivated primarily by white fears of black competition in the labour market. When, from 1883, white-owned newspapers took note of public disturbances started by whites' attacking black people, they reported them under headlines identifying the attacks as 'race riots'.[10] They evaded the question of responsibility for the disorder. The idiom of race suited white interests because it reinforced the black-white divide and invoked beliefs about inherited as opposed to learned differences. This idiom was employed as a form of white intellectual property. Race became a social category fundamental to a formalized and legal structure of segregation backed by criminal sanctions. It was much more than a reference to 'the races' as a simple denotation of blacks and whites.

Nothing illustrates this better than the landmark case of *Plessey v Ferguson*. Following a planned challenge to the state law, Homer Plessey was forcibly removed from a railway carriage reserved for white travellers under an 1890 act of the State of Louisiana. He petitioned the US Supreme Court, stating that he was of seven-eighths Caucasian and one-eighth African blood; that the mixture of coloured blood was not discernible in him; and that, possessed of the rights of a United States citizen, he had lawfully occupied a vacant seat. However, the Supreme Court upheld the constitutionality of the Louisiana law, denying that its 'separate but equal' provisions were 'unreasonable'. It held that 'the object of the [Fourteenth] Amendment was undoubtedly to enforce the absolute equality of the two races before the law, but in the nature of things it could not have been intended to abolish distinctions based on color'. Note that the judgment referred to just two races.[11]

In the early years of the twentieth century there were struggles within the black population over the most appropriate names to use. This was an era in which there were separate water fountains and toilets for 'white' and 'colored', and the latter name was commonly used. As some black intellectuals favoured the name Negro, there was a call in 1908 for a new civil rights organization, to be called the National Negro Committee. It was established in the following year under the name National Association for the Advancement of Colored People. The name, NAACP, and the inclusive expression 'people of color', have continued in use into the twenty-first century.

The expression 'race relations' first appeared in 1911. Mention of race continued to signify a reference to relations between blacks and whites. The same year also saw publication of the forty volumes of the

US Congressional Immigration Committee, the Dillingham Report. This has been described as the high point of political propaganda for immigration restriction.[12] It was followed, in 1916, by publication of Madison Grant's *The Passing of the Great Race*, and, in 1922, by the establishment of the American Eugenics Society under the intellectual leadership of C. B. Davenport. For a whole generation, typological notions of race, mixed with a selective interpretation of genetical inheritance, influenced educated opinion. The anthropologist Franz Boas stood out as its most vocal critic.

The one-drop rule for distinguishing blacks from whites was an element in a strategy by which whites, especially in the southern United States, and like the whites in South Africa, took five steps towards the construction of a two-category social system.[13] They tried to:

1. Establish a comprehensive system of racial classification;
2. Ensure that racial classification was the basis for determining a person's entitlements in as wide a range of situations as possible;
3. Institute sanctions to reward the obedient and punish the disobedient;
4. Institutionalize group rather than individual competition;
5. Permit and encourage the tendencies of socio-economic inequalities to be transmitted from one generation to the next.

In South Africa this was a conscious strategy, especially after 1948 when the National Party set about legislating apartheid. In the United States it was not a conscious strategy, but a critical component in the political programme of the segregationists in the Deep South; they had a disproportionate influence upon national policy.[14]

If the relations between peoples of different colour are seen as the outcome of transactions within a framework defined by legislation, it will be noted that among the reasons for the failure of attempts to enforce steps 2, 3 and 4, in both the United States and South Africa, was the difficulty experienced by those in power in getting members of the superordinate category to act in conflict with their personal interests. For example, there were whites in the Deep South who ran commercial establishments, like gasoline stations, and they wanted to sell to black as well as white customers. The costs of compliance imposed on the would-be seller could exceed the benefits, so that some relationships were defined as 'business' and were exempted from the colour code.

Another exemption was that federal agencies, like the mail services, would not or could not comply with the code. Also, machines either work or fail to work irrespective of the colour of the person operating them. The expectation that blacks should give way to whites became unrealistic when the parties were driving automobiles at more than 25 miles per hour.[15] Exemptions multiplied. The dividing line between black and white changed relations less than the increase in the number of situations that were exempted from its application.

The last of these steps also invites comment. The new society built after 1776 was to be inspired by 'the American dream' of social mobility, by which whites might move from log cabin to White House. However, as in other societies, successful people worked to give their children a 'good start in life'. Statistics suggest that the transmission of inequality from one generation to the next in the United States is not now greatly different from that in other industrialized countries.[16] This has been particularly important for blacks, since, in the intergenerational relay race that is social mobility, their arrival on the starting line was delayed. It was an addition to the list of handicaps with which they had to contend.

Discrimination

A book by George M. Fredrickson has cast light upon *The Black Image in the White Mind* as this existed between 1817 and 1914. The author chose an appropriate year in which to conclude his study, for World War I stimulated 'The Great Migration'. Close to half a million blacks had left the South by 1920 and they were joined by another three-quarters of a million by the end of the 1920s. This migration was 'great' by contrast with the relative immobility of blacks prior to the new century.[17] The black image in the northern white mind must have changed substantially once northern whites experienced the arrival of blacks as job seekers, house hunters and as parents wanting school places for their children. Discussion of these changes would be helped were there a corresponding study of the white image in the black mind.

Because blacks and whites were categorized as different races, this experience will have contributed to the fashioning of the distinctive US conception of race. Black immigration into the northern cities led to the creation, in many trades, of a split labour market and, in many cities, of split housing markets and divided school systems.

This introduces the question of discrimination, a word used in many senses. At the very minimum, it is necessary to compare the legal definition of discrimination with the philosophical conception, and to comment on its use in economic analyses.

The philosophical conception derives from Aristotle's discussion of justice.[18] It defines discrimination as 'the unlike treatment of like things'. There is then a problem of defining what things are alike.

Governments declare only some kinds of discrimination to be unlawful. The European Court of Human Rights recognized what might be considered lawful discrimination, but chose to call it differentiation.[19] It held that differential treatment may be permitted where there is: a reasonable and objective justification; the differential treatment is in pursuit of a legitimate aim; and there is proportionality between the effects of the measures and the objectives. According to a recent UN study[20]:

> Nowadays, it is universally accepted that the term 'discrimination' has to be reserved for arbitrary and unlawful differences in treatment. 'Distinction', on the other hand, is a neutral term, which is used when it has not yet been determined whether a differential treatment may be justified or not. The term 'differentiation', on the contrary, points to a difference in treatment, which has been deemed to be lawful.

In international law, the practice is to regard 'discrimination' as illegal by definition and to make an explicit distinction excepting from such a definition actions and policies like those called 'affirmative action' and 'positive action'. It is also necessary to specify the ground of an allegedly discriminatory action; there are various prohibited grounds, including discrimination on the grounds of age, gender, race, colour, ethnic origin and national origin.

To establish whether a person has been treated less favourably, it is necessary make a comparison. Because of this requirement, the legal prohibition of unequal treatment is in some respects narrower, and in other respects wider, than the philosophical conception. It is narrower because its prohibitions do not cover private life or permitted forms of unequal treatment. That it can be wider is exemplified in the Directive 76/207 of the European Union. This recognizes the legitimacy, in terms of the principle of equal treatment, of protecting a woman during and after pregnancy; so if an employer dismisses a woman because she is pregnant, this counts as sex discrimination, even though no comparison has been drawn with the treatment of a man who has to absent himself from work to obtain lengthy hospital treatment. Less favourable treatment on grounds of race and less favourable treatment on grounds of pregnancy are unlike when seen philosophically, but regarded as alike when seen legally.

In social science, the concept of disadvantage resembles the concept of differentiation in law. Any form of handicap associated with membership in a particular class of persons constitutes disadvantage. It can have many causes, of which discrimination is only one. For example, the children of immigrant parents who grow up in a household, and in a minority community, in which the language of the homeland is spoken in preference to the language of the country of settlement, may be at a disadvantage in their education. Not all their disadvantage can be attributed to discrimination, though it is possible that if the children's teachers assume that such children will respond less well to classroom lessons, that assumption might give rise to a form of discrimination.

In economics, difficulties arise because economists usually base their analyses on data collected, for their own purposes, by governments or other organizations. In the case of the United States, the argument about possible discrimination may therefore turn on inferences from figures (such as, for example, those on the Ratio of Black to White Family Median Incomes, or Black and White Labor Force Participation Ratios, etc.). While data is sometimes collected by 'audit' (arranging for blacks and white testers to apply for the same jobs or services), and experimental economics is a growing specialism, these are not the primary sources of the evidence used by economists. Nevertheless, a leading authority has insisted that despite the paucity of really hard evidence about the years prior to 1940, some of the common US assumptions can be shown to be false.

> Consider, for example, the widely held belief that the typical white employer discriminated by paying a lower wage to a black worker than to a white worker who did the same work. Employers were free of legal constraints on this form of discrimination, but the evidence indicates that they usually did not practice it.

The writer also went on to explain that the available evidence shows that there were so many forms of differentiation within the markets for obtaining employment, and then for advancing within various trades, that any analyses relying on an assumption of perfect competition are of little value.[21]

Nevertheless, some generalizations are possible. It seems clear that the black workers who took part in the Great Migration competed for employment primarily in the private sector; they progressed economically because they were offering employers valuable services and employers were looking for the best bargains in the labour market. For employers, ethnic background mattered less than the value of the services on offer. Black advances (in southern cities as well as in the North) had to be secured in the teeth of opposition from trade unions. Thus in 1891, Kansas enacted the first of what were called prevailing wage laws. It provided that 'not less than the current rate of per diem wages in the locality where the work is performed shall be paid to labourers, workmen, mechanics and other persons so employed by or on behalf of the state of Kansas' and was copied elsewhere, including by federal laws after 1927. Though black workers, fleeing from the southern system of share-cropping, were willing to work for less than the prevailing wage rate, these laws made it too expensive for employers to hire them. Black workers were willing to join unions, but most unions would not have them. So employers hired them to break strikes by white unions, which added to the racial prejudices of white workers. Legislation adopted as part of the New Deal in 1933–35 had a similar effect because it established codes that determined minimum wages. Implementation of the codes was policed by joint union-employer panels; once any wage differential was removed, some employers dismissed black workers and hired whites in their place.[22]

In some northern cities small numbers of blacks had lived side by side with whites, but once the number of blacks passed a threshold, relations changed. In 1909, in the middle-class area surrounding the University of Chicago, a neighbourhood-improvement association launched a drive to ensure that 'the districts which now are white ... remain white'. Where blacks had bought houses in such districts, the association bought property owned by blacks and offered cash bonuses to renters who agreed to move out. It boycotted local merchants who served the black residents who would not fall into line. Chicago is said to have been quite typical of northern cities with respect to the establishment of black-white residential segregation.[23]

Residential segregation meant that neighbourhood schools were predominantly black or white, and while no northern state governments required segregation, some allowed local communities to establish racially separate schools. Asked why they chose to move north, blacks who had taken part in the Great Migration often mentioned the better educational opportunities for their children.[24]

Some parts of the South continued for a long time to extend their legal provisions for separating blacks and whites. In 1930, Birmingham, Alabama, legislated to penalize them if they played dominoes or checkers together. Five years later, Oklahoma separated them while fishing or boating. Nevertheless, in the 1940s and 1950s the national economic gap between black and white narrowed even more than in the decades that followed.[25] The US army and navy were ordered to desegregate in 1950. In the next decade, some southern cities started to hire black police officers on equal terms with white officers. Then, in 1954, the colour line was undermined by the *Brown v Board of Education* decision that found school segregation to be unconstitutional. At the United Nations, 1960 was 'Africa Year'; the arrival in the United States of ambassadors from new black nations, wearing colourful African costumes, was a source of inspiration to African Americans. It also affected white perceptions; and when restaurants and hotels on the New York–Washington highway treated these ambassadors in the way that they treated black Americans, the State Department took fright.

Preoccupation with the one-drop rule attracted attention to the statistics about black-white differences at the expense of attention to the statistics about socio-economic differences within these two categories. By the 1960s, the black middle class had come to resemble the white middle class in respect of education and social mobility, while an impoverished section of the black population was becoming more socially isolated. This was the theme of a much-discussed study of the declining significance of the black-white distinction that ran alongside the increasing significance of the incorporation of the black population into the US class structure.[26]

There is always an interaction between the top-down forces of change in the wider world, and in the federal and state governments, as they encounter the bottom-up pressures – such as those exemplified in the Civil Rights movement, in new economic relations and in changing public attitudes. The bottom-up pressure led to the Civil Rights Act of 1964 and to further legislation that constituted what has been called 'the second Reconstruction'. This was pushed through by President L. B. Johnson, even though he knew that it would cause his party to 'lose the South for a generation'.[27] The 1964 Act mandated equal rights for individuals. In December 1971, during the Nixon

administration, guidelines were issued to make it clear that a spec-
ification of 'goals and timetables for the prompt achievement of full
and equal employment opportunity' issued in 1968 were meant 'to
increase materially the utilization of minorities and women'. Policy
shifted from the rights of individuals to the equalizing of social categories. The expression 'affirmative action' (which had been used by
President Kennedy in 1962) was revived to designate obligations laid
upon employers.[28]

The policy of affirmative action became an intellectual battleground,
fiercely defended as necessary to make amends for past injustices,
and equally assailed as creating new injustices. Critics insisted that
the number of blacks in higher-level occupations had been increasing
before the passage of the 1964 Civil Rights Act, and claimed that other
reductions of inequalities were simply continuations of pre-existing
trends. As a result of government regulation, the less-fortunate blacks
became worse off economically, while those already more fortunate
rose rapidly.[29] The proportion of black income going to the top fifth of
blacks increased, while that going to each of the bottom three-fifths
declined.

Economists would expect market pressures to reduce discrimination in private-sector employment, but to have less effect in the public
sector because public-sector employers are under less pressure to pay
the costs of discrimination. It is possible that up to the late 1960s there
was greater discrimination against blacks in public-sector employment, whereas since then there may well have been discrimination in
favour of minorities in the public sector.

Affirmative action programmes in admissions to the University of
California provide a striking example of how public-sector discrimination in favour of certain minorities, and against Asians and whites,
could be operated in a manner that made it difficult to ascertain just
what was going on. Ward Connerly, the man who advanced the proposal that gave rise to the 2002 ASA statement, was appointed a member of the Board of Regents of the University of California in 1993. A
year later, he was approached by two white parents who told him what
had happened to their son who, despite an outstanding academic record, had been unable to obtain a place in the University's medical
schools. On the bottom of all the University's official documents was
a statement that the University did not discriminate in terms of race,
color or background. Connerly started asking questions. In the following year he received, anonymously, a copy of the key document

stipulating how many more points white and Asian applicants had to secure if they were to gain admission. He, and others, concluded that the University was implementing, not a programme of 'affirmative action', but a system of racial preferences.[30] In 2003, Connerly helped place Proposition 54 on the California ballot; it prohibited the state government from classifying any person by race, ethnicity, color or national origin, with some exceptions, such as for medical research.

The One-Drop Rule

Black leaders at this time used the black-white division to promote black solidarity and to minimize the significance of colour differences within the black population. They took over the idiom of race (making extensive use of the idea of racism) as black intellectual property valuable in disputes with their opponents. The one-drop rule helped recruit a maximal constituency. F. James Davis has recounted the experience of persons of white appearance plus some sign of black ancestry. They were repelled by the special prejudice shown by some whites towards anyone whose very appearance challenged the assumption that blacks and whites were separate populations. On the other hand, these fair-complexioned persons could also be offended by blacks who accused them of trying to pass for white.[31] Many of them chose to identify as black. As a result, Davis could testify in 1991 that 'the one-drop rule is now as fully accepted in the black community as a whole as it is in the white community'.[32]

The 'racial divide' in 1900 was represented in the census returns, with whites accounting for 83.0 per cent of the recorded population and blacks for 12.3 per cent. The census of 2010 recorded a total US population of nearly 309 million persons. It divided this total to report, first, the number of 'Hispanic or Latino' persons (16.3 per cent; as opposed to 'Not Hispanic or Latino', 83.7 per cent). It then reported self-identification by 'Race'. Of the total population, 97.1 per cent reported only one racial origin; 72.4 per cent reported that they were White, 12.6 per cent that they were Black or African American, 17.1 per cent that they belonged in some other single race category and 2.9 per cent that they were of two or more races.

Thereafter the figures get more complicated because of the distinction between Hispanic origin and Race as census categories. Explaining the 2010 census form, it was stated, 'For this census, Hispanic origins are not races' because 'in the federal statistical system, Hispanic origin is considered to be a separate concept from race.' This did not prevent some individuals from self-identifying their race as Latino, Mexican, Puerto Rican or Salvadorian, etc.[33] The value of the figure of the number of persons of Hispanic origin who reported that they were of more than one race is reduced by this confusion.

The four categories involved in the largest 'multiple race combinations' were: White and Black (1.8 million), White and Some Other Race (1.7 million), White and Asian (1.6 million) and White and American Indian and Alaska Native (1.4 million). Two or more racial origins were reported by 3.2 per cent of Whites and 7.4 per cent of Blacks. California had the largest minority population (22.3 million), followed by Texas (13.7 million), New York (8.1 million), Florida (7.9 million) and Illinois (4.7 million).

By 2050 the percentages will have changed dramatically. The Census Bureau calculates that the non-Hispanic white population will be declining in numbers, and is unlikely to account for more than 52 per cent; Hispanics will be at least 22 per cent, more numerous than African Americans at 15.7 per cent. The fast-growing Asian and Pacific Islander population will have increased to 15.7 per cent, while the American indigenous peoples will number in the 1–2 per cent range. The picture will be very different from the divide of 1900. Other disparities, such as those of socio-economic status and equality of opportunity, will attract more attention, and before that time opposition to any collecting of data on 'race' in the current mode will surely have increased.[34]

Counter Trends

Statistics of race and ethnic origin can be misleading if they are not complemented by other statistics, including those that bear upon socio-economic status. A leading African American journalist, looking back on his own experiences, has insisted, 'There was a time when there were agreed-upon "black leaders", when there was a clear "black agenda", when we could talk confidently about "the state of black America" – but not anymore.'[35]

He contended that instead of one black America there are now four: a Mainstream middle-class majority with a full ownership stake in American society; a large, Abandoned minority with less hope of escaping poverty and dysfunction than at any time since Reconstruction's crushing end; a small Transcendent elite with such enormous wealth, power and influence to which even white folks have to genuflect; and two newly Emergent groups – individuals of 'mixed-race' heritage and communities of recent black immigrants. The four sections of the population are increasingly distinct, separated by demography, geography and psychology. They have different profiles, different mindsets, different hopes, fears and dreams. The four sections have become so distinct that they view each other with mistrust and apprehension, while remaining reluctant to acknowledge the depth of the divisions.

This is a national picture; local circumstances may be very different. Yet the differences within the 'black' category (consisting, according to the 2010 census, of 38,929,265 persons – much larger than the total population of many European states) challenge older ideas of the black-white divide. They also pose problems for the institutions that have to decide what statistics are to be collected and how. The Census Bureau cannot do this properly without clarity about the purposes for which figures are wanted.

These statistics may neglect some of the features of modern life that promote uniformity because they affect everybody and are so mundane that they can be overlooked in the discussion of social trends. Community distinctions are usually observed in the private sphere (notably in matters of religion), but life in both private and public spheres is powerfully influenced by technological changes, such as automobile use, public transport, computers, television (and the use of the English language), mobile phones, cash cards, the electoral system, taxation, etc. Such standard contingencies of social life reduce the impact of racial and ethnic distinctions.

This chapter has reviewed what academic sources report on the sources of contemporary US associations with the word 'race' without attempting to distinguish the many sources in question (among which mass media reporting and the cinema deserve special attention). It has launched a wider argument that this growth in practical knowledge has been fed into the intellectual straightjacket manufactured by the one-drop rule. This restriction has the consequence that in the contemporary United States the word 'race' carries too big a load of disparate meanings, many of them with strong emotional associations. The White House 'Initiative on Race' instituted by President Bill Clinton in June 1997 can be viewed from this perspective.[36] The Initiative asked the American people to join their president in a national effort 'to lift the burden of race', and created a seven-member Advisory Board that was chaired by the African American historian John Hope Franklin. Funded for just twelve months, the Board nevertheless attempted to examine all aspects of racial, ethnic and immigration relations as they affected major institutional sectors. It reported in September 1998.

One academic commentator has compared the Clinton Initiative with two previous national assessments. Myrdal's American Dilemma defined a postwar liberal orthodoxy on race that, first, denied the existence of intrinsic racial/cultural differences between blacks and whites, and, second, identified white racism as the most important barrier to black advancement. A generation later, the Kerner Commission report of 1968 sustained this orthodoxy while shifting attention from individual racism to institutional racism, in keeping with the times. Clinton's Advisory Board perceived racial/cultural differences as the crux of the problem because they threatened national unity. It reflected the ideological developments of the post–civil rights era.[37] Whatever view is taken of the Clinton Initiative on Race, it is surely testimony to the hold on the American mind of this peculiar conception of race, and to the conclusion that the popular conception has to be broken into separate components for any analysis of black-white and minority relations.

Brief though this chapter is in relation to its subject, it may suffice to explain how the American Sociological Association came to respond to a political initiative designed to halt the collection of information on race and ethnicity within California. In the situation in which they found themselves, members of the ASA had to employ the ordinary language, 'one-drop' conception even though it is at odds with scientific knowledge. Placing the two kinds of knowledge together created a paradox. The Association could not reflect upon all the changes in the political environment that had led to what appeared to be a threatening initiative. The reconsideration of the place of race and ethnicity in sociology had to be left as a task to be undertaken by specialists in the field.

Notes

1. For a fine account of the diversity of the sources of what by the middle of the nineteenth century had become the black population, the changes of one historical period to the next and the variations from one part of the country

to another, see Ira Berlin, *Many Thousands Gone: The First Two Centuries of Slavery in North America* (Cambridge, MA: Harvard University Press, 1998).

2. Winthrop D. Jordan, *White Over Black: American Attitudes Toward the Negro, 1550–1812* (Chapel Hill: University of North Carolina Press; New York: Harper, 1968).

3. For popular usage in England before 1800, see Roxann Wheeler, *The Complexion of Race: Categories of Difference in Eighteenth-Century British Culture* (Philadelphia: University of Pennsylvania Press, 2000), and Kathleen Chater, *Untold Histories: Black People in England and Wales During the Period of the British Slave Trade, c. 1660–1807* (Manchester: Manchester University Press, 2009).

4. Jordan, *White Over Black,* 481.

5. George M. Fredrickson, *The Black Image in the White Mind: The Debate on Afro-American Character and Destiny, 1817–1914* (New York: Harper 1971).

6. Park, in his preface to Bertram Wilbur Doyle, *The Etiquette of Race Relations in the South* (Chicago: University of Chicago Press, 1937), xxi.

7. James Davis, *Who Is Black?* (University Park: The Pennsylvania State University Press, 1991), 34–37.

8. Jordan, *White Over Black,* 44.

9. 60 US 393, para 24. See Ariela J. Gross, *What Blood Won't Tell: A History of Race on Trial in America* (Cambridge, MA: Harvard University Press, 2008), 22. For court decisions separating blacks from whites before and after 1865, see also Roberts, *Fatal Invention,* 14–19.

10. The earliest newspaper headline using the expression 'race riot' may have been that in the *Chicago Daily Tribune* for 10 August 1883, 'Sanguinary Race-riot'. Use of this expression enabled the newspaper to avoid assigning responsibility for the outbreak of the violence.

11. Not until 1987 did the Supreme Court put to rest any doubts about whether, in passing the Civil Rights Act of 1866, Congress intended to protect more 'races' than blacks and whites. Considering cases brought on behalf of a Jewish synagogue and a person of Arab origin, the Court then held that Jews and Arabs were among the peoples considered to be races when the statute was enacted. A distinctive physiognomy was not essential to qualify for protection. Discrimination based upon ancestry or ethnic characteristics could be racial discrimination in law (*107 Supreme Court 2019 & 2022*). In discussions of Supreme Court cases since 1987, references to actions 'on the basis of race' have usually been references to the one-drop conception of black-white differences.

12. Barkan, *The Retreat of Scientific Racism,* 83. On the eugenics movement in the United States, see Yudell, op. cit.

13. Michael Banton, *Ethnic and Racial Consciousness* (London: Longman, 1997), 88–104.

14. Ira Katznelson, *Fear Itself: The New Deal and the Origins of Our Time* (New York: Liveright, 2013), 223.

15. Charles S. Johnson, *Patterns of Negro Segregation* (New York: Harper, 1943), 117–138.

16. Statistics of inequality require constant updating, but two recent reports are notable: 'Using one-generation measures of social mobility – how much a father's relative income influences that of his adult son – America does half as well as Nordic countries, and about the same as Britain and Italy, Europe's least mobile places. America is particularly exposed ... because its poor are getting married in ever smaller numbers, leaving more children with single mothers short of time and money. One study suggests that the gap in test scores between the children of America's richest 10% and its poorest has risen by 30–40% over the past 25 years.' Miles Corak of the University of Toronto reckons that in the United States and the United Kingdom around 50 per cent of income differences in one generation are attributable to differences in the previous generation. Other studies by Gregory Clark at the University of California, Davis, suggest that 'even in famously mobile Sweden, some 70–80% of a family's social status is transmitted from generation to generation across a span of centuries' (*The Economist*, 9 February 2013, 13, 74). Measures of the intergenerational transmission of inequalities should not be limited to income inequalities. On the transmission of inequalities, some of which may be traced to medical stereotyping in the pre-1865 era, see Roberts, *Fatal Invention*, 81–103, 123–146.

17. Stephan Thernstrom and Abigail Thernstrom, *America in Back and White: One Nation, Indivisible* (New York: Simon & Schuster, 1997), 54.

18. Aristotle, *Politics*, book 3, section C.

19. Abdulaziz, Cables and Balkandali v. UK [1985] 7 EHRR 471.

20. *Prevention of Discrimination: The Concept and Practice of Affirmative Action.* Final report submitted by Mr. Marc Bossuyt, Special Rapporteur, in accordance with Sub-Commission resolution 1998/5. UN document E/CN.4/Sub.2/2002/21 paragraph 91(a). Alternatively, see Marc Bossuyt, 'Prohibition of Discrimination and the Concept of Affirmative Action', in *Bringing International Human Rights Law Home* (New York, United Nations, 2000), 93–106: 'For some time now, the term "discrimination", which has a definitely pejorative connotation, has been reserved solely for unjustified differences of treatment, whereas the term "distinction" is completely neutral. The term "differentiation", by contrast, designates a difference of treatment for which there are legitimate reasons.'

21. Robert Higgs, 'Black Progress and the Persistence of Racial Economic Inequalities, 1865-1940', in Steven Shulman and William Darity, Jr. (eds.), *The Question of Discrimination: Racial Inequality in the U.S. Labor Market* (Middletown, CT: Wesleyan University Press, 1989), 9–31. This volume reviews the debate about the economics of affirmative action as it stood in the 1980s.

22. Walter E. Williams, *Race and Economics: How Much Can Be Blamed on Discrimination?* (Stanford: Hoover Institution Publication 599, 2011), 32–35, 91–93.

23. Thernstrom and Thernstrom, *America in Back and White*, 58–61.

24. Ibid., 62.

25. Ibid., 69–96.

26. William Julius Wilson, *The Declining Significance of Race: Blacks and Changing American Institutions* (Chicago: University of Chicago Press, 1978).

27. The implementation of the 1964 Voting Rights Act has been cut back by the decision of the Supreme Court in the case of *Shelby County v. Holder* (USSC 12–16, 25 June 2013). See John Paul Stevens (Supreme Court Justice 1975–2010), 'The Court & the Right to Vote: A Dissent', *New York Review*, LX (13), 15 August 2013, 37–39, reviewing Gary May, *Bending Towards Justice: The Voting Rights Act and the Transformation of American Democracy* (New York: Basic Books, 2013).

28. Thomas Sowell, *Affirmative Action Around the World: An Empirical Study* (New Haven, CT: Yale University Press, 2004), 122–125. According to Gavin Wright, *Sharing The Prize: The Economics of the Civil Rights Revolution in the American South* (Cambridge, MA: Belknap Press and Harvard University Press, 2013), it was the enforcement of the 1964 Act's ban on discrimination in public accommodations that had the biggest effect in changing employment practices.

29. Thomas Sowell, *The Economics and Politics of Race* (New York: Morrow, 1983), 200–201.

30. Ward Connerly, *Creating Equal: My Fight Against Race Preferences* (San Francisco: Encounter Books, 2000), 130–134.

31. For example, Diane Watson, then a California state senator and later a congresswoman, said of Ward Connerly, 'He's married to a white woman. He wants to be white. He wants a colorless society. He has no ethnic pride. He doesn't want to be black' (*Creating Equal*, 77–78.) At one time Connerly was assigned security guards for his protection.

32. Davis, *Who Is Black?* 80, 127–132, 150–156, for examples.

33. Overview of Race and Hispanic Origin: 2010, *2010 Census Briefs*, issued March 2011, 5. The strange way in which the Office of Management and Budget incorporated the Hispanic/Non-Hispanic distinction into the federal statistical recording arrangements (see chapter 6) testifies to the strength of the one-drop rule upon the US conception of race. The political importance of the Hispanic identity required that some place be found for it. The growth of the Hispanic-identifying population will influence the future use of racial categories.

34. Ibid.

35. Eugene Robinson, *Disintegration: The Splintering of Black America* (New York: Doubleday, 2010).

36. John Goering, 'An Assessment of President Clinton's Initiative on Race', *Ethnic and Racial Studies* 2001 24(3): 427–484.

37. Claire Jean Kim, 'Clinton's Race Initiative: Recasting the American Dilemma', *Polity* 2000 XXXIII(2): 175–197.

3

International Pragmatism

The League of Nations had failed to prevent the outbreak of World War II, so while that war was still in progress, the allied powers planned the creation of a stronger organization to replace it. On Franklin Roosevelt's suggestion, it was to be named the United Nations. Upon ratification of its charter by the five then-permanent members of the Security Council – France, the Republic of China, the Soviet Union, the United Kingdom and the United States – and by a majority of the other forty-six signatories, the UN came into existence on 24 October 1945. Chapter XIV of the UN Charter established the International Court of Justice.

In 1945 the same states also established the United Nations Educational, Social and Cultural Organization (UNESCO). Its constitution declares: 'The great and terrible war which now has ended was made possible by the denial of the democratic principles of the dignity, equality and mutual respect of men, and by the propagation, in their place, through ignorance and prejudice, of the doctrine of the inequality of men and races.'

More importantly still, the international community started to create a legal foundation for a new world order. This began, in 1948, with the adoption of the Universal Declaration of Human Rights (UDHR). It was a standard-setting operation, formulating a 'common standard of achievement for all peoples and all nations'. The UDHR did not create any rights; instead, it recognized the existence of 'the equal and inalienable rights of all members of the human family'. It was given legal form later in the International Bill of Human Rights. This consists of the International Covenant on Economic, Social and Cultural Rights (ICESCR), the International Covenant on Civil and Political Rights (ICCPR) and the Optional Protocols expanding the ICCPR. These were all interstate treaties. States that became parties to them, as to other treaties, bound themselves to fulfil specified obligations.

As already mentioned, UNESCO in 1950 assembled the first of a series of four international committees of experts. This first committee agreed on a 'Statement on race' that affirmed, among other things, that 'the biological fact of race and the myth of "race" should be distinguished' and that 'it would be better when speaking of human races to drop the term "race" altogether and speak of ethnic groups'. The second committee, in 1951, issued a 'Statement on the nature of race and race differences'; this was followed, in 1964, by the 'Proposals on the biological aspects of race', and, in 1967, by the 'Statement on race and racial prejudice'. The 1996 'Statement on Biological Aspects of Race' of the American Association of Physical Anthropologists was published as the Association's revisions of UNESCO's 1964 statement. Other publications that formed part of UNESCO's 'programme of disseminating scientific facts designed to remove what is commonly known as racial prejudice' drew attention to the importance of research in Brazil for a global view of 'the race question'.

The Universal Declaration of Human Rights provided a framework within which the international community could, if it was so minded, recognize further rights and provide for their protection. One was the 1948 Convention on the Punishment and Prevention of the Crime of Genocide. It provided that any contracting party could call for action under the UN Charter for the prevention and suppression of acts of genocide.

The Racial Convention

At the end of the 1950s, alarmed by reports of attacks on synagogues and Jewish burial grounds in what was then colloquially known as 'West Germany', by Arab anxieties about policies in Israel and by the priorities of newly emerging states in sub-Saharan Africa, some states pushed for a legal prohibition of racial and religious discrimination. Their actions resulted in the General Assembly's adoption in 1963 of the UN Declaration on the Elimination of All Forms of Racial Discrimination. Then, a year later, the General Assembly voted unanimously to adopt the International Convention on the Elimination of All Forms of Racial Discrimination. It proved to be the first of a series of interstate treaties expanding the scope of human rights law. In advance of the ICESCR and the ICCPR, it introduced much more demanding provisions for its enforcement than those of the Genocide Convention.[1]

The International Convention on the Elimination of Racial Discrimination (ICERD) provided, in Article 9, that parties to the treaty should submit to the UN regular reports on the legislative, judicial, administrative and other measures that they had adopted to give effect to the Convention's provisions. It provided, in Article 8, that the states' parties should elect a committee of eighteen experts to examine their reports and to report annually on the outcome to the General Assembly.

Though those who negotiated the drafting of the Convention did not expect many states to ratify it, the number of states that have become parties to it has steadily risen: from 41 in 1970 to 107 in 1980, and 129 in 1990; by 2013, 175 of the UN's 193 member states had become parties. Adoption of the Convention was important to some of the UN's new African member states, for they saw it as an instrument in the struggle against South African apartheid. Indeed, a tendency developed at the UN to regard action of this kind as the intellectual property of the African Group of member states. In this political atmosphere there were states that ratified 'out of solidarity' with the Africans' struggle without appreciating the implications for their internal affairs of the many obligations they were undertaking.

For states of the Eastern bloc, ratification offered access to a forum in which to increase pressure for decolonization and to criticize the colonial powers, while on the Western side ratification was in the interest of those anticipating such tactics. Many states display an ambivalent attitude to this and other human rights treaties. Though they wish to put pressure on certain other states to secure adequate protections for racial minorities, they do not want to expose their own policies and actions to unfriendly criticism.

It was not until 1994 that, following the initiative of President Jimmy Carter, the US Senate conducted hearings on ratification. The assistant secretary of state for democracy, human rights and labor told the Senate that ratification was essential:

> First, by ratifying the Convention, we will be better able to hold other signatories to their commitments. We need no longer fear that in doing so we would be playing into the hands of geopolitical adversaries. Instead, we can use the Convention as a reference point in our bilateral dealings with states, and we will strengthen our position in multilateral gatherings.

The United States became the 141st state party in 1994, though its ratification was subject to very extensive reservations.[2]

For the purposes of the Convention, 'racial discrimination' is defined in Article 1, paragraph 1, as

any distinction, exclusion, restriction or preference based on race, colour, descent, or national or ethnic origin which has the purpose or effect of nullifying or impairing the recognition, enjoyment or exercise, on an equal footing, of human rights and fundamental freedoms in the political, economic, social, cultural or any other field of public life.[3]

It uses the word 'race' both to designate a large class of persons to be protected from discrimination, and as one of five subdivisions of that class.

Paragraphs 2 and 3 in Article 1 specify certain exceptions from the definition in the previous paragraph. These exempt distinctions drawn by states between citizens and non-citizens, including naturalization. Paragraph 4 states:

Special measures taken for the sole purpose of securing adequate advancement of certain racial or ethnic groups or individuals requiring such protection as may be necessary in order to secure such groups or individuals equal enjoyment of human rights and fundamental freedoms shall not be deemed racial discrimination, provided, however, that such measures do not, as a consequence, lead to the maintenance of separate rights for different racial groups and that they shall not be continued after the objectives for which they were taken have been achieved.

Article 2(1) specifies the obligations of states parties to the Convention. Its second paragraph describes a state's obligation, when the circumstances so warrant, to take, in the social, economic, cultural and other fields, 'special measures to ensure the adequate development and protection of certain racial groups or individuals belonging to them, for the purpose of guaranteeing them the full and equal enjoyment of human rights and fundamental freedoms'. The implications of this provision are spelled out in the Committee on the Elimination of Racial Descrimination's (CERD) general recommendation 32.[4]

Article 3 condemns racial segregation. It is a prohibition of all forms of racial segregation in all countries, whether arising from the actions of states or private persons; its reference to apartheid is only illustrative.

Article 4 obligates states parties to punish incitement to racial hatred and any assistance to racist activities (there is no reference to racism and this is the only use of the adjective 'racist'). In the opinion of CERD, 'The prohibition of the dissemination of all ideas based upon racial superiority or hatred is compatible with the right to freedom of opinion and expression.'[5] Some states made their ratification of the Convention subject to reservations designed to protect their interpretations of these freedoms.

Articles 5–7 specify obligations to protect the equal right to security of personal, political, civil, economic, social, cultural and other rights, together with obligations to compensate victims and to combat racial prejudices by educational and other means.

Implementing the Convention

From its first meeting in 1970, through to 1988, the work of the CERD was influenced by the tensions of the Cold War between the Eastern and Western blocs; in some quarters it was seen as an adjunct to the UN's decolonization campaign. To start with, committee members interpreted the Convention as allowing them to receive information from states parties only. They soon found that many governments did not appreciate the extent of the obligations they had assumed by becoming parties to the treaty. For example, in several Latin American countries citizens could vote in elections only if they understood the Spanish language. The Committee held that this less favourable treatment of those who spoke only indigenous languages constituted racial discrimination, and persuaded these states to amend their laws.

Since then, and like some other human rights conventions, the ICERD has come to be regarded as a 'living instrument'. Later generations have discovered in it underlying principles that can be applied to new problems. The CERD has proposed actions for the better implementation of the Convention that have been adopted without any formal decisions by the states parties. For example, it has invited states to send representatives to present state reports and to engage in dialogue with committee members. Though there is no mention in the Convention of such dialogue, it has become a central feature of UN practice. CERD has formalized standard guidelines for reports, eased the demanding requirement that states should report at two-year intervals and introduced procedures for recommending preventive and urgent action, including action when states fail to report.

After 1988, the Committee was able to agree that it should adopt 'concluding observations' expressing a collective opinion of state implementation of treaty obligations. Its members started to take note of information received from non-governmental sources and to use it as a basis for questions put to state representatives. In law, the expression 'ethnic origin' is not problematic. An individual is at liberty to nominate one or more of his or her ethnic origins. CERD's general recommendation that, after having examined state reports submitted under the ICERD, it 'is of the opinion that such identification shall, if no justification exists to the contrary, be based upon self-identification by the individual concerned' has been endorsed.[6] CERD encourages states to publicize within their jurisdiction the protections offered by the Convention and the outcome of the dialogue with the Committee.

More recently, it has improved the dialogue by publishing in advance of its meetings a list of the themes on which it wishes to concentrate during consideration of a state party's report. It has instituted a follow-up procedure, and publishes in its annual report observations received from the state concerning the Committee's concluding observations. Moreover, it has opened opportunities for non-governmental organizations within reporting states to present their separate views on how the Convention's provisions are being implemented.[7]

This process of dialogue has continued. For example, the newly democratic state of South Africa became a party to the ICERD in 1998. When its first report was considered in 2006, it was immediately apparent that the state's legislation did not fully conform to the state's obligations and that it needed to supply more detailed information on the population, and on conditions prevailing in the country that affected implementation of the Convention. Dialogue between the Committee and the reporting state is sometimes tense, as when reports from Israel are examined, but it is usually productive.

The most recent (2007) US report is a document of 114 pages, dense with information on what the ASA statement of 2002 called the 'primary social institutions' that regulate black-white relations in 'the criminal justice, education and health systems, job markets and where people live'. It began with the statement that 'the U. S. is a multi-racial, multi-ethnic, and multi-cultural society in which racial and ethnic diversity is ever increasing' and went on to report the racial and ethnic categories used since 1997 in the US census.

In its observations on the report, CERD recommended that the state ensure a coordinated approach for the implementation of the

Convention at the federal, state and local levels; that it strengthen its efforts to combat racial profiling; that it intensify its efforts to reduce residential segregation; and that it undertake further investigations into the causes of racial inequalities in education. Noting the stark racial disparities in the criminal justice system, it recommended further studies of the causes to determine the nature and scope of the problem and the implementation of remedial strategies; it made a similar recommendation with respect to the death penalty. It reiterated that states are under an obligation to guarantee equality between citizens and non-citizens in the enjoyment of their civil, political, economic, social and cultural rights. Further, it recommended that the state increase significantly its efforts to eliminate police brutality; that it review the laws that result in disfranchisement; that it recognize the right of Native Americans to participate in decisions affecting them; that it continue its efforts to reduce the persistent health disparities affecting persons belonging to racial, ethnic and national minorities; that it review the burden of proof in racial discrimination cases; and that it organize education programmes to make officials and the public in general aware of the provisions of the Convention.[8]

The United States responded to these observations with an account of the Department of Justice's multifaceted regulation of racial profiling, giving examples of court orders and settlement agreements about the collection of statistical data. In light of the Committee's concern about the detention and sentencing of juveniles, the United States provided further information on measures to ensure that the human rights of juveniles are protected and explaining that life imprisonment without parole was a lawful practice imposed in rare cases. Further information was provided on the support of individuals affected by Hurricane Katrina and on measures to make government officials, the judiciary, federal and state law enforcement officials, teachers, social workers and the public in general aware of the responsibilities of the state party under the Convention.[9]

By ratification, the United States exposed itself to international criticism and benefited from the opportunity to join in the evaluation of how well other states fulfil the shared obligations. This arises in the examination, under Article 9, of state reports, and, in a quite different way, under Article 14. The ICERD was the first UN human rights treaty to include a provision whereby a state party could agree to a procedure for individual complaints to be considered in Geneva. By 2012, fifty-four states had made the declaration under Article 14 allowing their citizens to petition the Committee if they claimed that their governments had not protected their rights as set out in the Convention. CERD considers, in private session, such complaints and the responses of the governments in question. In some cases it has found the complaints to be justified and has issued an advisory opinion to that effect. On such occasions the government has then recompensed an aggrieved person and taken action to prevent any recurrence. Neither the United States nor the United Kingdom has yet made a declaration under Article 14.

This provides the background to a new development in 2012. It relates to the compatibility of obligations under the ICERD with the rights to freedom of opinion and expression, and to differences in the ways in which countries police the borderlines. Germany, because of its past, is more ready than most countries to ban extremist political parties. France has a strict law governing the press. French policy was exemplified on 3 June 2008 when a court in Paris convicted, for the fifth time, the former film star Brigitte Bardot for statements that would not have attracted prosecution in many other countries. In a public letter to the president about the ritual slaughter of sheep that had not been stunned in advance, she had written 'Il y en a marre d'être menés par le bout du nez par toute cette population qui nous détruit, détruit notre pays en imposant ses actes' (which might be translated as 'one is fed up with being led by the end of one's nose by all these people who destroy us, and destroy our country, by imposing such practices upon us'). For incitement to racial hatred, she was fined 15,000 euros.[10]

In 2009, the German cultural journal *Lettre Internationale* published an interview with Thilo Sarrazin, the former finance senator of the Berlin Senate. He was quoted as saying, among other things, that

> The city has a productive circulation of people, who work and who are needed.... Beside them, there are a number of people ... who are not economically needed.... A large number of Arabs and Turks in the city ... have no productive function.... Large segments are neither willing nor able to integrate.... The Turks are conquering Germany just like the Kosovars conquered Kosovo: through a higher birth rate.... We have to completely restructure family policies: do away with payments, above all to the lower class.

In consequence, the Turkish Union in Berlin claimed to be a victim of the German government's failure to provide protection under Articles 2(1d), 4(a) and 6 of the ICERD.

There was an exchange of observations between the Committee, the state party and the petitioner. The state party maintained that, in law, the Turkish Union was not a victim, so its complaint was inadmissible; that freedom of speech could protect ideas that offend, shock or disturb others; and that the state's response had not amounted to any denial of justice. The Committee reached a contrary view, concluding that Mr Sarrazin's statements amounted to dissemination of ideas based on racial superiority or hatred, that the state party had failed in its duty to carry out an effective investigation into this possibility and that its failure amounted to a violation of the Convention. One member of the Committee (Mr Carlos Manuel Vázquez, a citizen of the United States) filed a dissenting opinion. He maintained that the complaint was not admissible and stated, 'Even if I agreed that Mr. Sarrazin's statements incited to racial discrimination or contained ideas of racial superiority, I would not agree that the State party violated the Convention by failing to prosecute him.'[11]

States differ in their readiness to allow an external body to pass judgment upon their actions in dealing with what they see as domestic obligations. They fear what is sometime called 'mission creep', that a treaty body may issue advisory opinions on matters state officials believe to be outside its competence. This would, in their view, intrude upon their sovereignty. Therefore when states nominate one of their nationals to serve as a judge on the International Court of Justice, the European Court of Justice, the European Court of Human Rights or the Inter-American Court of Human Rights, they nominate an eminent expert and that person receives a corresponding salary.[12]

Since the middle of the twentieth century, the UN has played the leading part in the creation of an international vocabulary for use in the definition and protection of human rights. The conception of race in the Convention is one designed to protect a human right; its meaning depends upon the context in which it is used and forms part of ordinary language usage. Whether the word 'racism' deserves a place in that vocabulary can be disputed.

Other International Action

The UN General Assembly, on a proposal from the USSR, first designated 1971 as the International Year to Combat Racism and Racial Discrimination, and then 'the ten-year period beginning on 10 December 1973 as the Decade for Action to Combat Racism and Racial Discrimination'; it did not consider what was gained by adding 'racism' to the definition of racial discrimination in the ICERD. The Assembly's failure to secure agreement on the meaning to be given to this word gave trouble soon afterwards.

At the General Assembly in 1975, the representative of Kuwait introduced Resolution 3379, declaring, 'Zionism is a form of racism and racial discrimination.' It was a major step in a campaign by Arab states against Israel and the movement, Zionism, which had created that state. The originators of the resolution did not draw any distinction between racism and racial discrimination; they saw the two as aspects of the same thing, in line with a description that is discussed in chapter 5. Supporters of the proposition argued that under Israel's law, only Jews could be proper citizens in Israel, and that, since Jews were a race, the Israeli state was racist.

Their arguments were criticized by Daniel Patrick Moynihan, the US ambassador to the UN, who was himself a social scientist. He quoted *Webster's Third New International Dictionary* that defined racism as 'the assumption that ... traits and capacities are determined by biological race and that the races differ decisively from one to another'. According to the dictionary, racism also involved 'a belief in the inherent superiority of a particular race and its right to domination over others'. Moynihan maintained that the assumption, and the belief to which the dictionary referred, were both alien to Zionism. He described this as a movement, established in 1897, that was to persons of the Jewish religion a Jewish form of what others called national liberation movements.

Moynihan followed the dictionary in insisting that 'racial discrimination is a practice, racism is a doctrine'. The UN had defined racial discrimination but not racism. The allegation that Zionism was a form of racism was 'incomparably the more serious charge'. When, earlier, the wording of a preambular paragraph to the ICERD was under discussion,

> The distinguished representative of Tunisia argued that 'racism' should go first because, he said, Nazism was a form of racism. Not so, said the so less distinguished representative of the Union of Soviet Socialist Republics, for, he explained, Nazism contained all the main elements of racism within its ambit and should be mentioned first. That is to say that racism was merely a form of Nazism.... If, as the distinguished representative

declared, racism is a form of Nazism, and if, as this resolution declares, Zionism is a form of racism, then we have step by step taken ourselves to the point of proclaiming – the United Nations is solemnly proclaiming – that Zionism is a form of Nazism.[13]

It will be noticed that the representatives of Tunisia and the USSR were relying on essentialist rather than nominalist definitions.

Each of the three decades culminated in an international conference at which political campaigning overshadowed consideration of better implementation of the Convention. The third of them was the World Conference Against Racism, Racial Discrimination, Xenophobia and Related Intolerance convened in Durban, South Africa, 31 August–8 September 2001.[14] The UN now conducts a periodic review of the implementation of the programme adopted at that conference. It has also established a Working Group of Experts on People of African Descent that follows up the conclusions of the International Year for People of African Descent in 2011.

Other global and regional international organizations have taken action to combat racial discrimination. Among them, particular notice should be taken of an initiative within the International Labour Organization. This was inspired by research undertaken in England in 1967–68 that had been instrumental in securing parliamentary approval for the extension of the prevailing anti-discrimination legislation. By measuring the frequency of actions of a racially discriminatory character when persons applied for employment, housing and financial services, the research had established that the incidence of racial discrimination was higher than had been believed (even by members of the black minority).

In Geneva in 1989, a programme, 'Combating Discrimination against (Im)migrant Workers and Ethnic Minorities' was started within the Migration Branch of the International Labour Organization.[15] Within this programme, the lead study, conducted in the Netherlands, found that in one out of every three responses to advertisements of vacancies for semi-skilled employment, a Moroccan applicant received less favourable treatment than a Dutch applicant. When job seekers had to apply by post, even immigrants who had received a Dutch college education and spoke Dutch fluently were seriously disadvantaged. The research in Belgium, Germany, the Netherlands, Spain and the United States all reported an incidence of discrimination not greatly different from that found in the Netherlands and the United Kingdom.

Studies were conducted into the efficacy of anti-discrimination legislation in ten countries and anti-discrimination training in six countries. These studies concluded that the criminal law is relatively ineffective in preventing discrimination in the workplace and in enabling its victims to obtain compensation. A study of British figures, where allegations of discrimination in employment are adjudicated under civil law, concluded that the laws against racial discrimination in employment were slightly more effective than the law against burglary, and that their effectiveness was not very different from that of the law against robbery.[16]

Within the UN, there are five regional groups of states: the African Group with fifty-four members, the Asia-Pacific Group with fifty-three, the Eastern European Group with twenty-three and the Western European and Other Group with twenty-eight, plus one observer (the United States).[17] There are other regional organizations, including the Organization of American States, with thirty-five members, the European Union (currently of twenty-nine states) and the Council of Europe with forty-seven. These regions have, or are planning, their own conventions, courts and other institutions for the protection of human rights. The Council of Europe in 1993 established the European Commission Against Racism and Intolerance (ECRI). This Commission examines reports from Council of Europe states on their implementation of their obligations as members of the Council. The examination is not conducted in public, as with the UN, but by teams of Commission members who visit states and discuss state reports with state officials and other bodies. ECRI then publishes its report.

Naming the Categories

As mentioned above, states that are parties to the ICERD submit periodic reports to the UN.[18] These show that countries vary in their conceptions of race and of ethnic group, and that they fulfil their treaty obligations in different ways. For example, the approaches adopted in the United Kingdom resemble those in the United States much more than the approaches adopted in France. In the United Kingdom up to the late 1950s, it was customary to draw a dividing line between 'white' and 'coloured', and the first proposal for legislation against discrimination bore the title 'Colour Bar Bill'. A decision to extend the scope of legislation to cover discrimination against Jews lay behind the Labour Party's adoption, in 1958, of the expression 'racial discrimination'. Trends in the United States (often taken up by West Indians in Britain) came to favour the idiom of race instead of colour. So did the mass media. In the 1960s, 'race' was a short but powerful headline word, signifying concern over New Commonwealth immigration, then it was used in connection with street disturbances, accusations of discrimination and so on. The UK government gave to its first law against racial discrimination the title Race Relations Act 1965. It has continued with this nomenclature in its 1968 and 1976 Acts and in subsequent amending legislation.

In the United Kingdom, what came to be called 'ethnic monitoring' was introduced in 1965 in order to ensure that no one school should have more than about 30 per cent of immigrant pupils. It was extended to the collection of data on employment, the allocation of social housing and to the provision of medical services. A parliamentary committee advised that whenever members of the public were requested to provide such information, the reason for the request should be given. The police introduced an 'identity code' for the identification of suspects, based on their appearance.[19]

When comparing experiences in different countries, it should never be forgotten that between 1939 and 1945 doctrines of racial inequality tore Europe apart. It is therefore not surprising that European states have long wanted to banish a mistaken conception of race. In preparation for the world conference at Durban in 2001, the fifteen states of the European Union stated their shared objection to any wording that might appear to endorse belief in the existence of different human races. This objection has been stated forcibly by the Swedish parliament, which in 1999 'declared that there is no scientific justification for dividing humanity into distinct races and from a biological standpoint consequently no justification for using the word race with reference to humans.... The government in international connections should try to see that usage of the word race with reference to humans is avoided in official texts so far as is possible.' Since 1994, Sweden has had a law against ethnic discrimination that covers racial discrimination, rather than the other way round.

In Africa, however, many governments are fearful of any expression that might exacerbate tensions between ethnic minorities, and they are reluctant to collect information on ethnic origin in statewide censuses. Nor do the conceptions of race and ethnicity held in the West have equivalents in many Asian countries. This is discussed in chapter 6.

Though the response of the American Sociological Association in 2002 may have revealed a paradox in its conception of race, there is no paradox in respect of international law. Any problems about the relation between things and words employ the ordinary language meanings of words like 'race' and 'ethnic origin'; these problems are dealt with in a legal framework, not a social science framework.

From an international perspective, the adoption of the ICERD, and the dialogue between the Committee and reporting states, have resulted in a great growth in practical knowledge about race and ethnicity and an impressive dissemination of that knowledge. It has drawn attention to the widespread incidence of discrimination in forms that members of majorities are inclined to regard as only 'natural', and shown how the circumstances of marginalized groups, such as the Roma, are to be addressed within the framework of human rights law.

Notes

1. Michael Banton, *International Action Against Racial Discrimination* (Oxford: Clarendon Press, 1986), 99–100.
2. For ratification by the United States and the reservations, see Michael Banton, *The International Politics of Race* (Cambridge: Polity, 2002), 98–102.
3. The distinction between 'purpose' and 'effect' was later drawn in US law in the Griggs case of 1971 by the differentiating 'disparate treatment' from 'disparate impact'; in the UK, the Racial Relations Act of 1976 similarly distinguished between 'direct' and 'indirect' discrimination and this was the terminology employed the European Union directive of 2000/43/EC.
4. A/64/18 Annex VIII.
5. CERD General recommendation XV of 1993 (UN document HRI/GEN/1/Rev.9, 279). Other general recommendations concern the rights of non-citizens, the rights of indigenous peoples, gender-related dimensions, discrimination against Roma, discrimination on grounds of descent, discrimination in the criminal justice system and hate speech.
6. General Recommendation VIII, 1990 (UN document HRI/GEN/1/Rev.9, 274).
7. Michael Banton, 'States and Civil Society in the Campaign against Racial Discrimination', *Nationalism and Ethnic Politics* 2012 18(4): 385–405.
8. In chapter 1 it was noted that US genomicists complain about their being obliged to employ racial categories defined by the US Office of Management and Budget. If these have not been already revised, the examination of the next periodic report of the United States would provide an opportunity for the US delegation to be questioned on their suitability.
9. UN document CERD/C/USA/CO/6/Add.1, 5 February 2009.
10. Retrieved 7 August 2013 from https://fr.wikipedia.org.
11. UN document A/68/18 Annex III, Decision concerning communication No. 48/2010.

12. Though members of UN treaty bodies exercise judicial functions, they are not remunerated accordingly, but receive an allowance for travel and subsistence expenses.
13. General Assembly records A/PV.2400, 152–165.
14. For an assessment of the conference, see Banton, *The International Politics of Race*, 142–169.
15. Believing that it might be a sensitive issue within the ILO, the research was initially funded by individual governments and trade union–linked foundations. Though eleven countries were invited to participate, in only Belgium, Germany, the Netherlands, Spain and the United States could the plans be implemented as intended. Because of the early death of the principal investigator, the findings were not publicized as widely or as well as might have been expected. The best account is that in Roger Zegers de Beijl, Irene McClure and Patrick Taran, 'Inequality in Access to Employment: A statement of the challenge', *UNESCO, United to Combat Racism* (Paris: UNESCO, 2001), 153–167.
16. Michael Banton, *Discrimination* (Buckingham: Open University Press, 1994), 59–61.
17. Israel has temporary membership in the Western European and Other Group.
18. These reports contain much information useful for the study of racial and ethnic relations. The United Nations Human Rights website, http://www.un.org/en/rights, leads to UN bodies – Charter-based and Treaty-based – and then to the Treaty bodies database; alternatively, the reader can go to http://tb.ohchr.org/default.aspx or the Official Document System, http://ods.un.org/.

    To minimize duplication when submitting reports under different human rights treaties, states are invited to submit a Core Document describing the state and the framework within which it protects human rights (e.g. for the USA, HRI/CORE/USA/2008); these documents can be very helpful. The United States' 7th–9th periodic reports are combined in CERD/C/USA/7–9; the summary record of the dialogue between CERD and the US delegation on these reports can be located on the second and third of these websites at CERD/C/SR.2299–2300, while the concluding observations are included in the annual report A/70/18.
19. Michael Banton, 'Ethnic Monitoring in Britain', in Andrea Krizsán (ed.), *Ethnic Monitoring and Data Protection: The European Context* (Budapest: Central European University Press, 2001), 252–264. The police 'identity code' had the following categories:
    IC1 – White person, northern European type
    I2 – Mediterranean European/Hispanic
    IC3 – African/Afro-Caribbean person
    IC4 – Indian, Pakistani, Nepalese, Maldivian, Sri Lankan, Bangladeshi or any other (South) Asian person
    IC5 – Chinese, Japanese or South-East Asian person
    IC6 – Arab person
    IC0, IC7 or IC9 – Origin unknown

4

Sociological Knowledge

Theoretical knowledge grows when there is a framework that synthesizes existing knowledge, pointing up gaps and problems that can stimulate new research. Thus Linnaeus, Darwin, Mendel, Fisher, Haldane, Wright, Crick, Watson, Venter and others built or modified frameworks for the biological study of human variability. In so doing they developed an appropriate theoretical vocabulary.

Theoretical or Practical?

Within the social sciences, the psychologists were first off the starting blocks when they used Freud's writing to develop the theory of frustration and aggression; they followed this with the study of stereotypes and of social attitudes, intelligence testing and the authoritarian personality. In 1954, Gordon Allport's *The Nature of Prejudice* launched a continuing series of experiments on the effect of personal contact upon intergroup attitudes; then in 1961, a book by Muzafer Sherif reported on his famous Robbers Cave experiments with groups of adolescent boys and formulated his 'realistic conflict theory'. Later came Henri Tajfel's 'social identity theory'. The point to note about these contributions is that they fostered the growth of theoretical knowledge about social interaction in general, including black-white interaction, without being dependent upon any concept of race.

A comparable advance in economics was heralded with the publication in 1957 of Gary Becker's *The Economics of Discrimination*. This used the economists' model of international trade to analyse the economic relations between blacks and whites in the United States. That is not the best kind of model for the analysis of imperfect competition and exposes it to the criticisms that have been outlined in chapter 2

The character of economists' contribution to the study of black-white relations is therefore better illustrated by a study published in 1995 about the relations between people who, in Chicago, sought to buy new automobiles and the men employed to sell them. It showed how, in that sector of the car market, considerations at the interpersonal level could decide aggregate outcomes.[1]

Those who conducted the experiments employed assistants, here called testers, who played the purchaser role. Black male testers inquiring about the possible purchase of particular vehicles were quoted prices $1,100 (or 9 per cent) higher than the prices asked of white testers. If the testers bargained, they could secure price reductions, yet the black-white disparity remained. Black female testers were quoted prices $280 higher than white male testers and, though the price was reduced in the course of bargaining, it finished $400 higher than the final offer made to white male testers for the same vehicle. Initial offers to white female testers were $55 higher than to white males, but the discrepancy in final offers increased to $130. Several factors apparently contributed to these findings.

An earlier study had found that many would-be purchasers believed that the prices quoted to them were not negotiable. In the Chicago study, 31 per cent of white purchasers and 61 per cent of black respondents believed this. Women were more likely than men to be misinformed about the willingness of dealers to bargain, though the gender discrepancies were not as great as those between blacks and whites. The research workers concluded that the main reason for the price differences was that dealers, wanting to make profits, drew their own conclusions about how much inquirers might be willing to pay (their 'reservation prices'), and, irrespective of whether the dealership owners or their sales representatives were black or white, they thought they needed to concede less to blacks and to females than to white males. Blacks, particularly black males, were disadvantaged by the dealers' images of them as customers, and this explained much of their disparate treatment.

Blacks and women were treated less favourably because sales representatives, wishing to maximize their earnings, took advantage of purchasers who knew less about how the market operated; they concealed the extent to which quoted prices were negotiable. If legal proceedings had been instituted, and charges had been brought against individual sales representatives, they would have been difficult to prove, though it would be possible, by law, to lay an obligation on their employers to see that all classes of customer were treated equally and then to bring charges of another kind.

In the attempt to account for observations such as these, a social science distinction has been drawn between categorical discrimination and statistical discrimination.[2] Categorical discrimination is the less favorable treatment of all persons assigned to a particular category. The black and female car purchasers were subject to statistical discrimination, i.e. less favorable treatment arising from a belief that people in a particular category are less likely to possess attributes that the discriminator is seeking. Thus it is generally believed that some employers, when considering whether to give employment to a young woman, will weigh the chances that before long the woman may be applying for pregnancy leave, so that a replacement will have to be found, and that replacement may require job training before she is of value to the employer equal to that of the woman she is replacing. The black and female would-be car purchasers were at a disadvantage because the sales representatives assumed them to be less well-informed about prices. (Racial disadvantage is any form of handicap associated with assignment to a racial category.) Children from minority families could experience statistical discrimination if their teachers believed that their academic potential was lower. In neither case is there any presumption that the belief is without objective justification.

For reasons that are not described in the article, the manufacturers of the automobiles apparently believed that, rather than announcing a fixed price, it was in their interest to allow their products to be marketed by a process of bargaining between sales personnel and potential purchasers. Had they wished to establish fixed prices they would presumably have needed to introduce a procedure for the oversight and sanctioning of sales personnel who, in pursuit of their private interests, broke the rules.

So, in economics, as in psychology, it is possible to analyse the buyer-seller relation in general, including black-white interaction, and to show that the same principles govern white discrimination against blacks, and male discrimination against females, without using any concept of race or gender. These emic constructs have been subsumed in more general conceptual frameworks based on etic constructs. The general frameworks convert categorical distinctions into variables, employing nominalist rather than realist definitions, and they can more easily measure the effects of causal influences. In retrospect, it would appear that sociological knowledge would have grown more rapidly had there been a stronger drive to construct a comparable generalizing framework for the explanation of what is sociologically distinctive about black-white relations. Later chapters will return to this critical contention.

The Chicago School

Twentieth-century sociologists inherited from their predecessors an emic conception of racial difference as influencing the relations between large populations. Starting in the 1920s, foundations for the sociological study of race relations were laid at the University of Chicago by Robert E. Park. Wanting sociology to become a natural science of human behaviour, Park began by seeking inspiration in the approach of biologists, particularly in their studies of ecology. So, to start with, he looked for causes underlying conscious behaviour. Together with Ernest W. Burgess, Park published *Introduction to the Science of Sociology* in 1921.[3] If it was to be recognized as a new subject, sociology had to offer something distinctive. So in this field it had to put forward an explanation challenging the assumption that group differences in behaviour were inherited in much the same way as differences in skin colour. The prevalence of such an assumption was documented in a study of how children reasoned. A researcher in education in the early 1920s gave some school classes the following silent reading test: 'Aladdin was the son of a poor tailor. He lived in Peking, the capital city of China. He was always lazy and liked to play better than to work. What kind of boy was he: Indian, Negro, Chinese, French or Dutch?' To his bewilderment, he found that many children in states close to the North-South border were so impressed by the statement that Aladdin was lazy that they answered that he must be Negro.[4] For the children, the description of Aladdin as Negro was more significant than the statement that he lived in China; they assumed that his laziness was inherited. If sociology had anything to say about 'racial relations', it needed to offer better explanations than this.

The early Chicago work started against the background of the city's race riot of 1919; this had led to the appointment of the Commission on Race Relations. Park wanted sociology to account for processes of communication, conflict, accommodation and interaction in human society. Society was conceived as an organization of persons by means of communication, socialization and collective behaviour; it was founded upon the ecological community as an aggregate of individuals characterized by symbiosis, the division of labour and competitive cooperation. Such a scheme was not obliged to incorporate the word 'race', but when Park came to apply his ideas, it slipped in unquestioned.

Among the new ideas contributed by Park was the notion of social distance: 'Everyone, it seems, is capable of getting on with everyone else, provided each preserves his proper distance.' On this basis, Emory S. Bogardus devised a social distance scale that could be used to measure majority attitudes towards members of minorities in the United States. In Zambia it was employed to measure intertribal attitudes, enabling the author to publish a table of 'Percentage of Northern Matrilineal Respondents accepting Africans of other groups of tribes in given relationships'.[5] The scale could have been elaborated to measure the maintenance of many forms of social distance, including those based upon gender, religion, socio-economic status, etc. This way, the study of distance between blacks and whites could have been subsumed within a larger framework had the sociological imagination risen to the opportunities.

Though Park encouraged empirical research, the measurement of behaviour, like the observance of social distance, was not a priority. Over the years, he came to put greater emphasis upon human consciousness as a determinant of behaviour, so that by 1939 he wrote that:

Race relations, as that term is defined in use and wont in the United States, are the relations existing between peoples distinguished by marks of racial descent, particularly when these differences enter into the consciousness of the individuals and groups so distinguished, and by so doing determine in each case the individual's conception of himself as well as his status in the community. ... Thus one may say, without doing injustice to the sense in which the word is ordinarily used, that there are, to be sure, races in Brazil – there are, for example, Europeans and Africans – but not race relations because there is in that country no race consciousness, or almost none. One speaks of race relations when there is a race problem.[6]

The significance of 'marks of racial descent' varied from one social situation, one country, and one time, to another. Their significance for members of minorities differed from their significance for members of majorities. To define a field of study in such terms was therefore a retreat from Park's initial aspiration to contribute to a natural science of human behaviour. It was an abandonment of any attempt to subsume the study of 'race' under the concepts of a more general explanatory theory and was a capitulation to the demands of ordinary language usage.

Park's reference to a 'race problem' echoed the way that white people used this expression to misrepresent a moral issue. Thus Gunnar Myrdal's book *An American Dilemma: The Negro Problem and Modern Democracy* concluded that white Americans faced a choice between the 'American Creed' of equal citizenship and the practices of their daily life.[7] So the United States faced a white problem. That the book's subtitle should have contradicted its main argument says much about the temper of the times.

How did the consciousness of 'racial descent' differ from the consciousness of assignment to a category based on ethnic origin? Park never properly grasped the sociological problem posed by the distinction between race and ethnic origin, even though his department was also famous for William Thomas and Florian Znaniecki's five-volume account of *The Polish Peasant in Europe and America*, a study that brought the ethnic dimension to the fore. Park's pupils were the prime contributors to a canon of works that set the parameters of the new field. This featured works by Charles H. Johnson, Franklin Frazier, Everett and Helen Hughes, Herbert Blumer and by some others who stood on the sidelines, including Lloyd Warner, John Dollard, Allison Davis and Oliver Cox. Together, these scholars built a tradition of inquiry and identified intellectual problems for research workers to tackle. One feature of this tradition has been the assumption that sociology should search – in the words of the US constitution – for a 'more perfect union'. It should help promote assimilation.

Whereas Park's frame of reference was usually the United States as a society, and often with processes of social change, W. Lloyd Warner was interested in how a local society could function when it was forcibly divided into black and white sections. He analysed black-white relations in the Deep South in terms of caste and class, a conceptual scheme that treated black-white relations as caste relations modified by distinctions of social class within both sections of the local population.[8] It contributed a detailed exposition of how social categorization was enforced in daily life.

In the post–World War II era, the main criticism of Park's and Warner's explanations came from Oliver C. Cox, who pioneered a Marxist interpretation. Agreeing with Park that race relations were the behaviour that developed among peoples who were aware of each other's actual or imputed physical differences, Cox insisted that the sociologist should specify the social circumstances in which that awareness arose. Racial consciousness was not inevitable: 'By race relations we do not mean all social contact between persons of different "races", but only those contacts the social characteristics of which are determined by a consciousness of "racial" differences. Two people of different "race" could have a relation that was not racial.'[9] Or he might have said that two persons with different physical and cultural characteristics can enter into relations that are not racially categorized.

Cox examined seven modern situations of free relationship between whites and persons of colour in which racial consciousness was generated: the stranger situation; the original contact situation; the slavery situation; the ruling class situation; the bipartite situation; the amalgamative situation; and the nationalistic situation. The United States exemplified the bipartite situation.

Having quoted Park's statement that there was no 'race problem' in the United States before the Civil War, Cox elaborated upon it:

> The race problem developed out of the need of the planter class, the ruling class, to keep the freed Negro exploitable. To do this, the ruling class had to do what every ruling class must do; that is develop mass support for its policy.... Race prejudice was and is the convenient vehicle ... [it is] the socio-attitudinal matrix supporting a calculated and determined effort of a white ruling class to keep some people or peoples of colour and their resources exploitable.[10]

He might well have added that the description of this consciousness as 'racial' suited the interest of the ruling class better than a description of it as a consciousness of colour difference.

His was a global vision, dramatized in the statement: 'If we had to put our finger upon the year which marked the beginning of modern race relations we should select 1493–94. This is the time when total disregard for the human rights and physical power of the non-Christian peoples of the world, the colored peoples, was officially assumed by the first two great colonizing European nations.'[11] Cox did not note that there here had been an Arab slave trade, from the eighth century onwards, that took into the Middle East and the Indian subcontinent almost as many men and women from East Africa as the Atlantic trade took men and women westwards.[12] Yet had he done so he would have been able to argue that the Arab trade could not have the same consequences because its control of slave labour power did not become part of a capitalist economic system.

Cox maintained that hostility towards Jews and the oppression of blacks served different social functions, were differently motivated and fitted into different parts of the capitalist system.[13] Therefore they did not pose the same sociological problems.

In World Perspective

In 1954 a conference on Race Relations in World Perspective was convened in Hawaii.[14] Dedicated to Robert Park, the conference brought together some forty social scientists and administrators selected for their knowledge of 'what happens when people of different racial backgrounds meet'. In retrospect it can be contended that what the sociology of race relations most needed was a conceptual framework in which race was subsumed within a more general theory of the creation and maintenance of social bonds and divisions. That had to remain a long-term aspiration, because, inevitably, the conference papers fell far short of any common sociological perspective.

Though Park had been particularly interested in what might be learned from the study of black-white relations in Brazil, the conference participants had to acknowledge that their 'emerging discipline' was obliged to take its lead from research into the US 'race problem', and that this had been 'largely conceived in terms of the Negro; in Latin America it dealt with the relations between Indians and whites; while in other parts of the world it was concerned with the "native"'. The editor regretted that the comparisons and generalizations that 'constitute the essence of science' have 'as yet only slightly penetrated into studies of race relations'.

The 'emerging discipline' was necessarily conceived in a manner that took US experience as the paradigm example of 'race relations', although this had drawbacks that were underlined by the participant who warned, 'In the study of race relations the student has crossed his pons asinorum when he has learned to define his "races" afresh for each new situation he is called upon to discuss.'[15] (The pons asinorum or 'bridge of asses' invoked by Maurice Freedman is the test of ability designed to assess the competence of beginners.) Freedman was referring to the different definitions employed in the countries of Southeast Asia when they counted the size of their Chinese populations, but his argument was of much wider application. As emic constructs, the meanings given to 'race' and 'ethnicity' varied from place to place and time to time. This problem was not properly addressed.

One of participants was J. S. Furnival, from 'the Ministry of National Planning, Rangoon, Burma'. He was the author of two books, *Netherlands India: A Study of Plural Economy* and *Colonial Policy and Practice*, in which he had launched a claim that Java and Burma in the years before World War II were examples of a 'plural society', 'a society, that is, comprising two or more elements or social orders which live side by side, yet without mingling, in one political unit'.[16] The 'elements' he had in mind were those classified by the Dutch as Europeans, Foreign Orientals and Natives. His conference paper did not discuss this concept, but since it later became very influential and described a perspective very different from that of Park, it invites comment at this point.

An Australian historian, Charles A. Coppel, later re-examined the evidence for the period and found much that was inconsistent with Furnival's account.[17] At that time one in five of the marriages contracted by European men in Java were with an indigenous or a Chinese wife. Furnival himself was married to a Burmese woman. Those classed as 'European' 'included the Eurasian population as well as Indonesian Christians, and "non-Europeans" could legally become "Europeans" (or be equated with them) in various ways. Illegitimate children of a non-European mother could become European by acknowledgement by the father, and where a European man married a non-European woman, she and her husband acquired European status.' There were many indications of social intercourse between these supposedly separate 'elements'.

The 'highly-acculturated peranakan Chinese of Java' were a living disproof of Furnival's assertion that the Chinese group held 'by its own religion, its own culture and language, its own ideas and ways'. Most of the peranakan were of mixed ancestry, spoke Malay and were unable to read (or even speak) Chinese. Their conversion to Islam had been 'quite widespread'. Later, many became Christians. In the period before 1910 there were some two hundred publications in Malay written by Chinese alone. Coppel therefore concluded that Java was not a 'plural' but a mestizo society, employing an expression used in the Philippines to describe persons of mixed ethnic origin. To classify Java and Burma as 'plural societies' was to overlook the structure of political power and to take insufficient account of a socio-economic status structure common to societies being drawn into capitalist economic relations.

Many authors (the present author included) were insufficiently critical of the conception of a plural society. Furnival was an economist by training and it might have been better had he written about the plural economy as administered by colonial governments. The word 'society' is an emic construct often used to designate the population of a state; there is no agreed method in sociology for differentiating 'society' from 'state' or for classifying different kinds of society. By representing the society as responsible for intergroup conflict, the conception of a plural society distracted attention from the political responsibility of individuals at the various social levels.

The Hawaii conference volume opened with an essay aspiring to provide 'a necessary framework of basic concepts and hypotheses' prepared by Herbert G. Blumer. He distinguished seven 'major lines of social relations in group life' without referring to any particular countries. Blumer was a leading exponent of the symbolic interactionist perspective that had been pioneered by Park's colleague George Herbert Mead. He began with the declaration that 'the term "race" is fundamentally a biological concept', which suggests that he had not talked much with the biologists at his university. Blumer insisted that, despite any biological ideas, people viewed and acted towards one another on the basis of social conceptions of race, and that these did not coincide with classifications made by physical anthropologists on the basis of biological traits. For this reason, social scientists had shifted to a social conception of race, such that they observed the relations between categories of people and sometimes found it instructive to classify them together as 'racial' even when the people themselves employed ethnic or religious rather than racial categories.

Social Race?

The anthropologist Charles Wagley had led the way in launching a conception of 'social race'. Studying a community in the Amazon basin where there was considerable admixture of European, African and Amerindian inheritance, he found that, in classifying one another, people paid more attention to a person's hair than to any other physical character.[18] There was, apparently, a scale of socio-economic status in which hair was most important attribute. Why then call this 'race'?

Wagley brought with him a scientifically unjustifiable US assumption that classification by 'race' was a universal mode of classification superior to classification by any particular phenotypical character. In referring to a 'social conception of race', Blumer was adopting a similar assumption.

Nor did Blumer show any awareness of Cox's arguments when, having asked, 'How do a given people come to be regarded as a race?' he went on, 'This question has not been studied, as far as I know, chiefly because it has not been posed as a scholarly problem.' He offered some conjectures that might contribute to an answer. Blumer did not acknowledge that whereas members of the general population in most countries used proper names (like Hausa, Ibo and Yoruba in Nigeria) to identify social categories based on ethnic origin, in the United States they used comparable proper names to identify subdivisions of the categories black and white. It was this practice that Warner had followed.

Though, for its time, Blumer's statement was a valuable contribution, it helped popularize the assumption that there can be a social concept of race, and it therefore helped create the paradox that was described in this book's introduction. Blumer failed to mention that use of the word 'race' in the United States had a history, or to ask which set of people were responsible for the usage he described. The dimension of power was neglected.[19]

How were these problems reflected in US undergraduate teaching? In 1966 Peter Rose conducted a comprehensive survey. The information collected persuaded him that most courses were ethnocentric, in that they concentrated on United States material and viewed the issues through American eyes. They were 'infused with an aura of scientific certainty as well as an undercurrent of moral indignation' such that tensions were presented as 'blemishes on the fabric of American society which must be understood, then eradicated'. The teachers did not present race relations 'in the context of such basic concepts as "power" or "conflict" or "alienation", but stressed the uniqueness of their concerns and the special nature of [US] racial problems'.[20]

The political environment was about to change, as the Civil Rights movement in the United States gathered strength, and as in 1968 students in many Western countries challenged the prevailing conceptions of social order. So it is apposite to pause over two student texts published in 1967 in order to review what constituted knowledge about 'race relations' in that year. At the outset, it may be noted that the expression 'race relations' (or 'racial relations') was employed only reluctantly because the connection between 'race' and 'relations' was questionable. Nevertheless, the expression had come into widespread use and there was no convenient alternative to it.

In the view of one author, there was by this time widespread agreement that the study of race relations brought together three approaches.[21] First, there was an approach from ideology that used racism as its basic concept. This was defined as the doctrine that a person's behaviour was determined by stable inherited characters deriving from separate racial stocks having distinctive attributes and usually considered to stand to one another in relations of superiority and inferiority. Second, there was an approach from attitude that used prejudice as its basic concept. Its essential features were its emotional character and its rigidity. Third came the approach from social relationships, based upon the concept of discrimination. It was the differential treatment of persons ascribed to particular social categories.

These were nominalist definitions. Racism was identified with typology, the pre-Darwinian doctrine outlined in the introduction, because this was the clearest example of a biologically based doctrine of racial inequality. It distinguished a specific doctrine from others with which it might be confused. Prejudice was defined in such a way that the expression of an attitude could be explained as the outcome of a disposition that could be measured on an objective scale. Acts of discrimination could be explained as the outcome of a choice between the costs and benefits of alternative ways of behaving.

The second author defined racism as 'any set of beliefs that organic, genetically transmitted differences (whether real or imagined) between human groups are intrinsically associated with the presence or absence of certain socially relevant abilities or characteristics, hence that such differences are a legitimate basis of invidious distinctions between groups socially defined as races'.[22]

Both books described situations that might be thought to constitute 'race relations'. The first book described seven: peripheral contact, institutionalized contact, acculturation, domination, paternalism, integration and pluralism. The second compared 'paternalistic and competitive types of race relations', identifying similarities and differences between Mexico, Brazil, the United States and South Africa, with particular attention given to the 'dimensions of pluralism'. Both, therefore, focused on the way in which the larger social institutions influenced interpersonal behaviour. Both employed what had been identified, six years earlier, as an 'oversocialized conception of man'.[23]

This conception developed a top-down perspective that analysed the pressures on individual behaviour, but paid insufficient attention to bottom-up social processes whereby individuals engage in collective action and change institutional structures.

The difficulty of inter-relating top-down and bottom-up processes has sometimes been called the 'micro-macro problem'.[24] One resolution of this problem, insofar as it arises in interpersonal relations, is to identify the multidimensionality of those relations. To elaborate: relations between A and B can be conducted on the basis of many relationships. They can be relationships of gender, age, religion, socio-economic class, language and so on. Such distinctions may be used to create categories (e.g. whether old enough to qualify for a licence to drive a car) or be variables. They may interact, as in the way that a perception of a class difference may be modified by a perception of a person's age. Much may depend upon the circumstances that may cause a party to become aware of a social difference as relevant to the business at hand. The social significance of a distinction will in practice be much more differentiated than the kinds of category employed in a research questionnaire.

The significance attributed to a difference in ethnic origin will be loaded by the persons' previous experiences and by the opinions of his or her peers. For some persons, a sentiment of solidarity with those who live in the same local community may include a feeling that this community has precedence over other communities. For example, studies conducted in African and Asian countries have reported that groups distinguished by ethnic origin may believe that they are owners of the local territory, and therefore have prior claims.[25] In Europe, there are groups based on ethnic origin who believe that they constitute the *staatsvolk*, the majority people, whose customs and expectations have established norms with which immigrant minorities should conform. In the United States, descendants of those whites who had settled before the mid-nineteenth century sometimes expressed sentiments of this kind, and Native Americans could make a similar claim, but, basically, the United States was an immigrant society and the territorial dimension to social claims was weak.[26]

The methodological principle is therefore that all macro distinctions will be present in micro relations, even if some of them are of little practical significance and may be difficult to locate.

A reference to a passage in a published book usually counts as evidence of what constituted knowledge at the time, but there are general understandings among those who work in a field that may not find a way into academic publications. Thus it can be suggested that, by the late 1960s, many sociologists would have agreed that when two persons met they would have seen each other's physical appearance, or phenotype, but not their 'race'. Physical characteristics stimulated a first-order abstraction; to infer from them that the other person belonged in a racial category was to make a second-order abstraction. It was this second abstraction that was conditioned by the social environment.

This 'social conception of race' was a forerunner to the description of race as a social construct in the 2002 ASA statement.[27] Many authors have remarked that 'race' is important not in itself but because it is associated with social differences of major significance. Thus the present author, in his 1967 book, preferred to argue that race (or phenotypical appearance) served as a role sign, an indicator of expected behaviour.

This argument could have been better related to the analysis of social interaction that had been outlined in an account of 'Social Behaviour as Exchange' by George Homans.[28] The approach from exchange set out to uncover a transactional basis to interpersonal relations; it maintained that, consciously or not, individuals acted so as to secure maximum net advantage. The costs and benefits to them might be either material (as in cash payments) or psychological (as in emotional satisfaction gained by the fulfilment of a duty as opposed to the cost implicit in a feeling of guilt). A person might recognize a norm, but observe it in practice only so far as the anticipated benefits of observance exceeded the costs.[29] When a research problem is formulated in terms like these it is easier to test a hypothesis and to reach an explanation. However, this perspective has not so far been much used in sociological studies of racial and ethnic relations.

This chapter has discussed the principal ways in which the first generation of sociologists specializing in the study of racial relations worked to build a body of theoretical knowledge. That was their mission as sociologists, even if at times they joined in the search for practical knowledge. Some may wonder whether the great increase in practical knowledge had been matched by a comparable increase in theoretical knowledge. Such a question permits no simple answer because the two kinds of knowledge are not commensurable.

Notes

1. Ian Ayres and Peter Siegelman, 'Race and Gender Discrimination in Bargaining for a New Car', *The American Economic Review* 1995 85(3): 304–321.

2. Michael Banton, 'Categorical and Statistical Discrimination', *Ethnic and Racial Studies* 1983 6: 269–283.
3. Robert E. Park and Ernest W. Burgess, *Introduction to the Science of Sociology* (Chicago: University of Chicago Press, 1921). The statement that Park 'conceived of sociology as a natural science of human behaviour' is taken from Burgess's article on Park in the 1970 edition of the *Encyclopaedia Britannica*. The contributions of the Chicago school have been discussed by many commentators. One recent critic is Stephen Steinberg, *Race Relations: A Critique* (Stanford: Stanford University Press, 2007). Like many others, Steinberg is critical of the very notion of 'race relations'. Insofar as it identifies a field of study, Steinberg believes that its mission is to accumulate practical knowledge and to present it in ways that will maximize the opportunities for applying it to problems in public policy.
4. Bruno Lasker, *Race Attitudes in Children* (New York: Henry Holt, 1929), 237.
5. See Michael Banton, *Race Relations* (London: Tavistock, 1967), 315–333. For the psychological research, see Harry C. Triandis, Earl Davis and Shin-Ichi Tazekawa, 'Some Determinants of Social Distance among American, German, and Japanese Students', *Journal of Personality and Social Psychology* 1965 2(4): 540–551. For an example of recent research, see Willem Huijnk, Maykel Verkuytem and Marcel Coenders, 'Family relations and the attitude towards ethnic minorities as close kin by marriage', *Ethnic and Racial Studies* 2013 36(11): 1890–1990.
6. Robert Ezra Park, *Race and Culture* (Glencoe: The Free Press, 1950), 81–82.
7. Gunnar Myrdal et al., *An American Dilemma: The Negro Problem and Modern Democracy* (New York: Harper, 1944).
8. W. Lloyd Warner, 'American Caste and Class', *American Journal of Sociology* 1936 (XLII) 234–237): 225. Warner's use of caste in the Mississippi situation is sometimes taken as drawing a parallel with Hindu caste, but it should be noted that the word 'caste' was sometimes used in the South in the nineteenth century to identify group boundaries.
9. Oliver C. Cox, *Caste, Class and Race: A Study in Social Dynamics* (New York: Monthly Review Press, 1948), 320, 475.
10. Ibid., 353–376.
11. Ibid., 475.
12. Ronald Segal, *Islam's Black Slaves* (London: Atlantic Books, 2002).
13. Cox, *Caste, Class and Race*, 393.
14. Andrew W. Lind (ed.), *Race Relations in World Perspective: Papers read at the Conference on Race Relations in World Perspective, Honolulu, 1954* (Honolulu: University of Hawaii Press, 1955). An earlier book that was particularly important in calling attention to the different outlook in most of the countries of Latin America was Frank Tannenbaum's historical study, *Slave and Citizen: The Negro in the Americas* (New York: Knopf, 1946).
15. Maurice Freedman, 'The Chinese in Southeast Asia', in Lind (ed.), *Race Relations in World Perspective*, 388–411, at 388. For the way in which 'race' was used in the census of Malaya, see ibid., 59–60.
16. John S. Furnival, *Netherlands India: A Study of Plural Economy* (Cambridge: Cambridge University Press, 1939), 446; *Colonial Policy and Practice: A*

Comparative Study of Burma and Netherlands India (Cambridge: Cambridge University Press, 1948).

17. Charles A. Coppel, 'Revisiting Furnival's "plural society"', *Ethnic and Racial Studies* 1997 20(3): 562–579. References to pages 567 & 575.

18. Charles Wagley, *Race and Class in Rural Brazil* (Paris: UNESCO, 1952), 122.

19. Herbert Blumer, 'Reflections on the Theory of Race Relations', in Lind (ed.), *Race Relations in World Perspective*, 3–21.

20. Peter Rose, *The Subject is Race: Traditional Ideologies and the Teaching of Race Relations* (New York: Oxford University Press, 1968), 68, 153–154.

21. Michael Banton, *Race Relations* (London: Tavistock, 1967), 7–8. For criticism, see Julian Pitt-Rivers, 'Race Relations as a Science: A Review of Michael Banton's *Race Relations*', *Race* 1970 11(3): 335–342, and the assessments of eleven reviewers in *Current Anthropology* 1969 10(2–3): 202–210. For self-criticism, see 'Finding, and Correcting, My Mistakes', *Sociology* 2005 29(3): 463–479.

22. Pierre L. van den Berghe, *Race and Racism: A Comparative Perspective* (New York: Wiley, 1967).

23. Dennis H. Wrong, 'The Oversocialised Conception of Man in Modern Sociology', *American Sociological Review* 1961 26(2): 183–193.

24. Theories in sociology, as in economics, have to resolve what is sometimes called the 'micro-macro problem', accounting for the interaction of top-down and bottom-up processes. One notable success was Allison Davis, Burleigh B. Gardner and Mary Gardner, *Deep South: A Social Anthropological Study of Caste and Class* (Chicago: University of Chicago Press, 1941). At the same time, Max Gluckman also demonstrated how the macro could be seen at work on the micro plane; see *Analysis of a Social Situation in Modern Zululand*, Rhodes-Livingstone Paper 28 (Manchester: Manchester University Press, 1958), reprinting an article in *Bantu Studies* 1940 14: 1–30, 147–174. The relative merits of the top-down and bottom-up perspectives was one of the components of the famous *Methodenstreit* that began in 1883 when Carl Menger, the founder of the Austrian school of economics, attacked the approach of the German historical school of economics represented by Gustav von Schmoller.

25. E.g. Donald L. Horowitz, *Ethnic Groups in Conflict* (Berkeley: University of California Press, 2000 [1985]), 138, 202, 209–211.

26. The expression *Staatsvolk* featured (in a non-ethnic sense) in Georg Jellinek, *Allgemeine Staatslehre*, 3rd. edition (Berlin: Springer, 1921 [1900]).

27. Over-use of the notion of a social construct has been criticized: Ian Hacking, *The Social Construct of What?* (Cambridge, MA: Harvard University Press, 1999).

28. George Homans, 'Social Behavior as Exchange', *American Journal of Sociology* 1958 63: 597–606.

29. This approach has sometimes been called rational choice theory, a name that has misled some commentators. It is a theory of all kinds of action, not only those that may be accounted rational; it simply tries to ascertain the costs of suboptimal decisions. It has to consider what alternative courses of action are available to an actor.

5

Conceptions of Racism

Supporters of the US Civil Rights movement of the 1960s brought concerns over black-white relations in that country to the centre of public attention. In 1967, two proponents of 'Black Power', Stokely Carmichael and Charles Hamilton, highlighted the exercise of power in the naming of social categories by recalling an often-quoted passage in Lewis Carroll's *Through the Looking Glass*. In it Humpty Dumpty declares, 'When I use a word ... it means just what I choose it to mean.' Because they lacked this power, 'black people have been saddled with epithets'. In *Black Power: The Politics of Liberation in America,* the authors described racism as 'the predication of decisions and policies on considerations of race for the purpose of subordinating a racial group and maintaining control over that group'.[1] They combined ideology, attitude and social relationships in a description that suited their political objectives. It was designed to illuminate the way that blacks were subordinated in the US political system.

According to Carmichael and Hamilton, racism took two forms, individual and institutional. They may have thought that, for their purposes, no definition of the second form was needed, for they observed only that it 'originates in the operation of established and respected forces in the society'. Over thirty years later, when a British judge was charged to conduct the Stephen Lawrence Inquiry, he sought a practical definition of institutional racism. He wanted to characterize the deficiencies he had uncovered in his inquiry into the investigation by the (London) Metropolitan Police of a racially motivated murder.[2] To this end, he wrote:

'Institutional Racism' consists of the collective failure of an organisation to provide an appropriate and professional service to people because of their colour, culture or ethnic origin. It can be seen or detected in processes, attitudes and behaviour which amount to discrimination through unwitting prejudice, ignorance, thoughtlessness, and racist stereotyping which disadvantage ethnic minority people.

This was a later elaboration, one intended to serve a purpose different from Carmichael and Hamilton's. Many of the arguments brought forward by them and other supporters of the Civil Rights movement were cogent; they inspired political reforms in the United States and changes in the political vocabulary of English-speaking countries.

The word 'racism' (which had its own history[3]) came to designate the contemporary attitudes, beliefs and practices that the Civil Rights movement sought to change. It entered ordinary, everyday language, and the Carmichael and Hamilton description was taken as a definition. 'Racist' was no longer simply an adjective used by scholars to identify an abstract doctrine; instead, it became a word in popular use employed as a moral accusation that could be thrown against political opponents. Its value as an epithet contributed to an inflation in its use, so that its meaning may no longer depend upon any belief about race. The nature of racism is often treated as self-evident. Its presence, persistence and effect are the things to be explained (the explananda).

Writing History

In chapter 1 it was claimed that sometimes a commentator wants a realist definition that seeks to grasp the most essential quality of the thing in question; at other times he or she wants a nominalist definition that distinguishes the thing from other things with which it might be confused. Any review of the definitions of racism in the academic literature has to conclude that most of them are of political inspiration and of a realist character. Thus, some historians have searched for the origins of racism in earlier centuries. They have assumed that there is a thing that corresponds to the word. That was no problem for Carmichael and Hamilton, for there was no doubt about the thing or things their movement sought to change. For a historian, though, there is a philosophical problem.

To look for the origins of something recognized only in the present is to read the past in the light of later ideas. The interpretation of historical periods in terms of the concepts, values and understanding of the author's own generation is known as presentism. It is a form of anachronism that has been a continuing weakness in many historical studies of human origins and human divisions. One illustration is to the fore in a book by a respected historian, George L. Mosse. He began with the declaration: 'Any book concerned with the European experience of race must start with the end and not the beginning: 6 million Jews killed by the heirs of European civilization, by a bureaucracy which took time out from efficiently running the state to exterminate the Jews equally efficiently and impersonally. How could this come to pass?'[4]

To start with an end is to presume that there could have been no other conclusion. It is as if Sir Isaac Newton were to be held in part responsible for the atom bombs that in 1945 were dropped on Hiroshima and Nagasaki. All too easily, a history that starts from the present overestimates the power of ideas and underestimates the responsibility of the people who have made use of those ideas.

Other examples merit the more attention because they can be found in the works of leading scholars. Thus, in *The Forging of Races*, Colin Kidd maintained that the historian has to explain 'the intellectual universe which justified slavery, segregation and imperialism'.[5] His point of departure was a summary of some modern findings in genetics, intended to inform his examination of 'the ways in which scripture has been mobilised in the pursuit of certain theories of race' and 'the ways in which the apparent "facts" of race threatened the intellectual authority of Christian scripture'. No one then knew what genetics would later discover, and since no new determinant of thought on such matters had been discovered, the intellectual universe that justified slavery had to be explained by reference to contemporary assumptions.

Another striking example can be seen in the work of Robert Bernasconi. Having assumed that there is 'a scientific concept of race', he asked, 'who invented it?' As an answer he pointed his finger at the philosopher Immanuel Kant, a man who wrote in the latter part of the eighteenth century when no 'scientific concept of race' existed. Kant nevertheless worked in a crucial period in which several scholars were wondering whether such a concept might open a path to the explanation of human differences.[6]

Some historians have ranged much further back than Kidd and Bernasconi, searching the records of classical antiquity for evidence of antipathies evoked by differences in physical appearance. Three have found little or nothing.[7] Their work may be contrasted with a fourth study that defined racism as an attitude that posits a direct and linear connection between physical and mental qualities; an account of the evidence found when using this definition enabled the author to fill over five hundred pages.[8]

Most histories of racism start not from a definition of racism, but from a description of racism as conceived in the historian's own time and circumstances. If there were an etic definition of racism it might be possible to investigate its causes and the results of the investigation might have policy value. Without any such definition, there is trouble. Thus a leading US historian, George M. Fredrickson, at one time avoided using the word 'racism' because he sought a 'usable past' and 'racism' was 'too ambiguous and loaded a term to describe my subject effectively'. He was looking for an alternative conception that embodied the values to which he felt committed, and later found it in the expanded meaning given to the word as a result of the Civil Rights movement. This satisfied him that the word 'racism' remained politically 'relevant' to scholars and activists.[9] His endorsement of a popular usage was an attempt to appropriate it for a political cause.

Fredrickson identified 'the two main forms of modern racism – the color-coded white supremacist variety and the essentialist version of anti-Semitism'. The earlier account of the 1975 UN discussion about Zionism should have drawn attention to some of the difficulties in referring to 'forms' of things that have been defined in essentialist terms. Fredrickson maintained that 'the responsibility of the historian or sociologist who studies racism is not to moralize and condemn but to understand this malignancy so that it can be more effectively treated'.[10] Some sociologists would agree with Oliver Cox that hostility towards Jews and the oppression of blacks serve different social functions and therefore are not the same 'malignancy'. Much has been changed by the creation of the state of Israel. For many people, anti-Semitism may no longer be part of what they understand by racism.

Fredrickson concluded that racism was 'a historical construction' that had existed in at least a prototypical form since the fourteenth and fifteenth centuries. Even if the word 'race' was not used, there could be 'equivalents' of biological determinism. Fredrickson treated racism as a thing that 'expresses itself', that 'sustains or proposes' and produces 'manifestations'. He observed that 'to achieve its full potential as an ideology, racism had to be emancipated from Christian universalism'. It is unlikely that Fredrickson would have believed that, over the centuries, events 'had to' develop as they did, but his choice of words bore such an implication.[11]

Mosse wanted to account for the Holocaust and identified racial ideas as exerting a causal influence. Fredrickson held that American institutions do not operate in the way they are supposed to operate and that ideologies were partly responsible. A very different interpretation of the motivation behind his and some other histories of racism sees it as springing from the whites' drive to redeem their sense of racial guilt. It is said that whereas racial slavery and segregation were built upon the stigmatization of blacks, the Civil Rights movement gave blacks the power to stigmatize whites for historical injustices. The shame was the greater because the notion of a distinctive American identity was founded upon a commitment to shared principles and political ideas. Corporate America is said to feel particularly vulnerable to accusations of racism.[12]

While the political functions of definitions of racism should be open for examination, it will be objected that any examination will also express some political position. This is true insofar as every statement can, in the last analysis, embody a political view even if it is a decision to disregard political struggles. The last analysis can be a long way off. Many mainstream sociologists sympathize with Weber's view that while 'it is the investigator and the prevailing ideas of the time that determine what becomes the object of investigation', once the research has started there is a standard to be met. A methodologically correct form of proof has to be logically correct. To point up the requirement that the explanation be culture-free, Weber insisted that it must hold true in the eyes of a Chinese scholar as well.[13] It must have the quality of cogency, such that even those who are opposed to it recognize that it has to be taken seriously on its own terms.[14]

In many quarters, the distinctions between racism and racial discrimination, ethnocentrism and xenophobia have been disregarded. Some sociologists currently describe people as 'experiencing racism' when they could more usefully identify the specific forms of discrimination and disadvantage from which the people may have suffered.

Teaching Philosophy

In 1689, John Locke prefaced his *An Essay Concerning Human Understanding* with the observation that great work in the advancement of knowledge was made possible by the preparations of the 'under-labourer in clearing the ground a little, and removing some of the rubbish that lies in the way to knowledge'. Peter Winch referred to this doctrine when contending that it was a mistake to believe that the role of the philosopher was limited to ground-clearing. He maintained that, while a main component of the philosopher's task was indeed the clearing up of linguistic confusions, that clearing up was relevant only insofar as it threw light 'on the question how far reality is intelligible'.[15] Without examining what social scientists actually do, he asserted that their mission was that of understanding, not explanation.

As Locke himself found, questions about language are central to the study of knowledge. In the search for understanding, and for its communication, ordinary language is usually more effective than technical language. In the search for explanation, and its communication, technical language opens paths to new and more profound knowledge, and to its possible applications.

Winch's little book had a particular importance because, as Ernest Gellner observed, it was the working out of the implications for the social sciences of Ludwig Wittgenstein's mature philosophy.[16] Moreover, according to Gellner, it constituted 'the best, most elegant and forceful, if quite unintended, refutation of Wittgenstein – one far more forceful than any stated by a deliberate critic'! It was condemned by its anthropomorphism, idealism and relativism.

Some teachers of philosophy, particularly in the United States, have recently approached these questions by starting from the meaning given to the word 'race' in the minds of their students, instead of from the intellectual problems in the field. Thus the editor of the volume *Race and Racism* in the Oxford Readings in Philosophy series starts his introduction with, 'Racial classification today is commonplace.' He goes on to argue that 'Europeans invented the idea of race for what appeared to them to be sound scientific reasons'; that 'the races, as we know them, are ... social constructions ... but it does not follow that biological races do not exist'.[17] As a result of the approach adopted, in his introduction the notion of an 'idea of race' is made to carry much too heavy a weight. The word is used in too many senses and, for US readers it will usually be infected by the assumptions behind the one-drop rule (for example, the reference to changes that enabled 'Jews and Arabs to become white' relies on a white/non-white distinction extending this rule).[18] The approach leads to a search to find who was responsible for inventing an idea that has done so much damage in the United States. It looks as if such teaching responds, probably unconsciously, to a sense of white guilt prevalent among the students attending classes on the philosophy of race.

The entry of the philosophers into this field may help correct the inability of many sociologists to perceive and examine the epistemological assumptions that underlie their reasoning. In stating the case for an approach from the perspective of critical rationalism, this book hopes to draw attention to some of those assumptions. It has tried to break up the problem as perceived in the Oxford Readings into a series of smaller problems to the solution of which philosophers might well contribute.

Teaching Sociology

In 1980, UNESCO extended its earlier programme by publishing a volume of essays, *Sociological Theories: Race and Colonialism*, that was in some respects a successor to the volume *Race Relations in World Perspective* of 1956. Many of the essays were characterized by what to the undergraduate student would appear abstract theorizing.

Several contributions reflected a move to formulate, within the tradition of historical materialism, a less deterministic model of racial discrimination than that which had been pioneered by Oliver Cox. They continued the work of Louis Althusser and Étienne Balibar, known as 'structural Marxism'.[19] One of them, Stuart Hall, warned against 'extrapolating a common and universal structure to racism' as if this remained 'essentially the same, outside of its specific historical location'. He went on to state, 'It is only as the different racisms are historically specified – in their difference – that they can be properly understood as "a product of historical relations and possess ... full validity only for and within those relations".[20]

Robert Miles, though starting from similar premises, could not accept this conclusion. He objected that if there were such 'historically-specific racisms', they must also have 'certain common attributes which identify them as different forms of racism.... Hall does not specify what the many different racisms have in common qua racism.' Miles's view was simpler: that class interests structure and stratify the labour market, encouraging the development of ideologies supportive of the ruling class. Racism is such an ideology, one that moulds popular conceptions of race, racism and racial relations. In Marx's terms, these exemplify 'phenomenal form' and are not part of 'essential relations'. Since both race and race relations are ideological notions used in ordinary language, sociologists are advised to focus instead on the study of racism.[21]

Yet Miles found definition of racism a far from simple task. His proposed solution was to draw upon the functionalist element in Marxist theory so as to hold that when biological differences are given social significance, this initiates a process of racialization. A popular belief in inherited differences associated with phenotype enabled a ruling class in a capitalist society to advance its interests by dividing the opposition. When ideas about cultural differences served the same function they could be treated as equivalent to ideas of 'racial' difference. There could be 'racism' even when no reference had been made to biological notions of 'race'.

> I use the concept of racism to refer to a particular form of (evaluative) representation which is a specific instance of a (wider) descriptive process of racialization. As a representational phenomenon, it is analytically distinguishable from exclusionary practices. Such a distinction is essential to the task of explanation because it does not foreclose the identification of the reasons why racialized populations occupy disadvantaged positions in contemporary or past social formations.[22]

Within the conceptual framework of historical materialism, this extension of the use of racialization can be justified, though there are serious difficulties if evidence of discrimination in Europe against Gypsies (Roma), against the Burakumin in Japan or between persons classed as Catholic and Protestant in Northern Ireland is to be regarded as evidence of racism. Perhaps for this reason, Miles and a co-author have since qualified this argument, in order to hold that when cultural characteristics lead to group formation and reproduction, the process is one of ethnicization.[23] This change undermines Miles's original use of the argument from functional equivalence. What should be very clear, however, is that the injunction 'do not study race relations, study racism!' is not an endorsement of study based on ordinary language conceptions of racism. Posing as a solution to one problem, it creates another.

If racism is based on beliefs about racial differences, and ethnocentrism on beliefs about ethnic differences, then an '-ism' based on beliefs about cultural differences would be better identified as culturism. However, current language usage sometimes takes a different course.

References to 'cultural racism' appear to be attempts to trade on the negative associations of racism.

The best way to resolve these conceptual problems would be to examine the purpose for which words like 'racialization' and 'racism' are used and see whether any other words can do the job more effectively. This is rarely done. Instead, some authors have tried to distinguish different explananda. With the expansion in the meaning of racism to include practices and actions, use of the word 'racialism' has been revived to denote theories or doctrines of racial inequality.[24] In France, *racisme* may be used to denote behaviour, and *racialisme* to denote doctrines of biological difference; doctrines of cultural difference may be called differentialist.[25]

Sociological Textbooks

Though the difference between racial discrimination and the expanded definition of racism is of the greatest importance for the formulation of social policy, it receives little attention in many US textbooks of sociology. It is even more notable that many authors, instead of offering a definition of the racism that is so central to what they have to say, provide instead examples of what they intend when they use the word. Or they describe things they consider racist.

For example, in a popular textbook, Joe Feagin has written:

> We will examine briefly some key aspects of systemic racism, including: (1) the patterns of unjust impoverishment and unjust enrichment and their transmission over time; (2) the resulting vested group interests and the alienating racist relations; (3) the costs and burdens of racism; (4) the important role of white elites; (5) the rationalization of racial oppression in a white-racist framing; and (6) the continuing resistance to racism.[26]

No criteria are provided by which it might be possible to determine whether a pattern of unjust impoverishment was racist or not. 'Systemic racism theory' is a body of theoretical writing built around a model of certain related practices in one country alone; it does not itself constitute a theory.

In another widely used textbook, Michael Omi and Howard Winant regretted that, since the mid-1960s, 'clarity about what racism means has been eroding', so that there is 'an overall crisis of meaning for the concept today'.[27] This is a comment on the way the word is used in ordinary language; it does not address the question of whether it has explanatory value in sociology. For that, the authors propose a concept of a 'racial project' and state that such a project 'can be defined as racist if and only if it creates or reproduces structures of domination based on essentialist categories of race'. They add, 'There is nothing inherently white about racism'. The authors' concerns are with the current state of black-white relations in the United States rather than with the growth of sociological knowledge as here described.

Some sociologists, while starting from ordinary language usage, attempt to give it greater precision and make it fit into their interpretive schemes. To their commitment to the advance of knowledge they add a competing commitment to the advancement of those forms of knowledge that are compatible with their political objectives. Assuming that their readers share with them a post-1967 ordinary language conception of racism, they offer a description of what it does instead of a definition. Thus, one author who criticizes 'common sense' conceptions, asserted: 'Because racism changes and develops, because it is simultaneously a vast phenomenon framed by epochal historical developments, and a moment-to-moment experiential reality, we can never expect fully to capture it theoretically. Nor can we expect that it will ever be fully overcome'.[28] If this claims any more than that societies change, and social practices with them, then there should be an indication of what defines racist practice. Another sociological authority has similarly stated: 'I reserve the term racism (racial ideology) for the segment of the ideological structure of a social system that crystallizes racial notions and stereotypes'.[29] These statements conceive of racism as something defined by its political functions. They run the risk of reifying racism. Moreover, on this line of reasoning, it might be expected that every distinct political position would have its own definition of racism.

A volume titled *Anatomy of Racism* assembled nineteen essays. In the editor's words, 'Each is committed in its own fashion to cutting up the body of racist discursive practices and expressions, stripping them to reveal the underlying presuppositions, embodiments of interests, aims and projections of exclusion and subjection. Each engages in short in the practices of what in the title to this collection I call "anatomy"'.[30] None of them defines the body in question. That so many authors, elsewhere as well as in this collection, advance no definition, suggests an awareness that their arguments would be damaged were they to attempt to do so. Similarly, the Oxford University Press commissioned a little book on racism for its Very Short Introductions series. Unsurprisingly, this job-definition encouraged the author to start from the word itself instead of from the purpose that the word has to serve. He sought to provide an 'understanding', assuming that anti-Semitism and 'anti-Irish sentiments' were part of what had to be understood.[31]

That it may be impossible to formulate a nominalist definition is suggested by the difficulties encountered by the sociologist who set out to distinguish 'everyday racism' from racism. 'Everyday racism' is said to involve 'only systematic, recurrent familiar practices' (like those of a hotel receptionist registering a guest). The author thought that a working definition of racism, had, however, to combine the macro with the micro: 'Racism then is defined in terms of cognitions, actions, and procedures that contribute to the development and per-petuation of a system in which Whites dominate Blacks.'[32] To say that something is defined in terms of a, b and c is no definition when the relations between the various terms are not specified. A nominalist definition takes the form 'X is ...', and not 'X includes ...' or 'X refers to. ...'

Nor is a realist definition of help in the analysis of discrimination by whites against minorities other than blacks, or of racial discrim-ination by blacks. That these forms of discrimination share certain features of white discrimination against blacks in the United States encourages use of the expression 'racisms', in the plural. The legiti-macy of any such extension must depend upon a demonstration of functional equivalence; current practice in the use of the plural con-ception often depends upon a politically contentious conception of the nature of the social system of which it forms a part. Yet a reputable publishing house can publish an introductory textbook titled *Racisms* that fails even to indicate that there are problems in the use of the plural.[33]

Arguments about 'racism' have continued, some under the rubric of Critical Theory and others within Cultural Studies. Critical Theory assembles criticisms of writing about 'late modern social and political life' that pay insufficient attention to 'racial conditions and racist ex-pressions'.[34] The Cultural Studies perspective is sceptical of claims to objective knowledge about social affairs, attempting to uncover, and criticize, any political assumptions underlying such claims. Thus it starts from the criticism of popular ideas rather than from the identification of sociological problems, which is why many of its exponents find ordinary language concepts sufficient for their purposes.[35] This approach prioritizes the reporting and interpretation of personal experience and seeks understanding rather than explanation.

Political Ends

The introduction of this book proposed, when assessing the controversies over race and ethnicity, to judge them by their value in leading to better explanations. This chapter must reach the conclusion that current conceptions of racism have been fashioned to serve political ends. Within the political sphere, the expanded conception of racism has highlighted popular consciousness of the legal and moral dimensions of behaviour, and has often been used as an epithet. However, the failure to differentiate the theoretical from the ordinary language vocabulary has spread confusion. The tendency for so many academic writers to rely on their own favoured conceptions, ignoring the philosophical issues, has led to extravagances. In the view of one critic: 'Few concepts in social science have been as diluted in content through overuse, as contaminated by the political agenda of the users, and as befuddled by multiple, indeed, sometimes contradictory, meanings as the term "racism".'[36] Critics object, for example, to the assumption that racism is a majority characteristic, so that, by definition, a victim of racism can never be considered a racist.

The introduction maintained that the growth of knowledge about phenotypical variation in humans had been made possible by the development of a theoretical knowledge distinct from practical knowledge. This chapter has to conclude that the recent popularity of racism in sociology books has contributed nothing to any growth of knowledge about the causes of social differentiation because it has refused to recognize any distinction between research directed to political ends and the kind of research that seeks explanations so cogent that they have to be accepted by persons with different political commitments.

The presentation of racism as a general cause of discrimination has distracted attention from the case for examining evidence of racial inequalities to see if they are the product of discrimination. When the sources of discrimination can be identified, it may be possible to rectify them by legal action. These considerations may help explain why the 2002 ASA statement 'On The Importance of Collecting Data and Doing Social Scientific Research on Race' nowhere uses the word 'racism'; nor does this word feature in the titles of any of the forty-four references cited in support of that statement.

Notes

1. Stokely Carmichael and Charles V. Hamilton, *Black Power: The Politics of Liberation in America* (Harmondsworth: Penguin, 1969 [New York, 1967]).
2. Sir William Macpherson of Cluny, *The Stephen Lawrence Inquiry*, vol. 1 (London: Home Office, 1999 CM 4262-1), 213–214.
3. By 1954 the word 'racism' was coming into use. In its French form, *raciste* was first used in 1894. Then, in 1933–34, the German sexologist Magnus Hirschfeld wrote articles about *Rassismus* that were later translated and published in 1938 under the title *Racism*. For sociologists, the first author to make important use of this concept was Ruth Benedict. Her book *Race: Science and Politics* (New York: Modern Age, 1940) was given the title *Race and Racism* in its London edition in 1942. As she was primarily concerned to correct misleading notions of the anthropology of race, she wrote that 'racism is the dogma that one ethnic group is condemned by nature to congenital inferiority and another group is destined to congenital superiority'.
4. George L. Mosse, *Towards the Final Solution: A History of European Racism* (London: Dent, 1978), xxv.
5. Colin Kidd, *The Forging of Races: Race and Scripture in the Protestant Atlantic World, 1600–2000* (Cambridge: Cambridge University Press, 2006), 1–2, 81.
6. Robert Bernasconi, 'Who Invented the Concept of Race? Kant's Role in the Enlightenment Construction of Race', in Robert Bernasconi (ed.), *Race* (Oxford: Blackwell, 2001), 11.
7. Frank M. Snowdon, Jr., *Before Color Prejudice: The Ancient View of Blacks* (Cambridge, MA: Harvard University Press, 1883); Lloyd A. Thompson, *Romans and Blacks* (London: Routledge, 1989); Ivan Hannaford, *Race: The History of an Idea in the West* (Baltimore: Johns Hopkins University Press, 1996).
8. Benjamin Isaac, *The Invention of Racism in Classical Antiquity* (Princeton: Princeton University Press, 2004).
9. George M. Fredrickson, *The Comparative Imagination: On the History of Racism, Nationalism, and Social Movements* (Berkeley: University of California Press, 1997), 6, 80, and *Racism: A Short History* (Princeton: Princeton University Press, 2002), 46, 47.
10. Fredrickson, *Racism*, 6, 158.
11. Ibid., 151.
12. Shelby Steele, *A Dream Deferred: The Second Betrayal of Black Freedom in America* (New York: HarperCollins, 1998), 119, 148. Note also the author's comments (121–122) on a bestselling book of an earlier generation: John Howard Griffin, *Black Like Me* (New York: Houghton Mifflin, 1961). This gave an account of the experiences of a white man who, having had his skin

chemically darkened, travelled the South passing for black. Steele says that the book put off many blacks because 'its very premise tended to mistake the black stigma for the entire black experience ... white America was invited not to see black life but to be aghast at it. However, the book's greater sin was to suggest that even if whites were morally obligated to support equality, race was still a problem that affected others.'

13. Max Weber, 'The "objectivity" of knowledge in social science and social policy', in Sam Whimster (ed.), *The Essential Weber: A Reader* (London: Routledge, 2004), 383, 365, 389.

14. This is the standard employed in those courts in which judges have to decide whether to allow an appeal against a court decision. The case for a rehearing has to be 'arguable'.

15. Peter Winch, *The Idea of a Social Science and its Relation to Philosophy* (London: Routledge, 1958), 3–11.

16. Ernest Gellner, *Cause and Meaning in the Social Sciences*, edited by I. C. Jarvie and Joseph Agassi (London: Routledge, 1973), 47–77.

17. Bernard Boxill (ed.), *Race and Racism* (New York: Oxford University Press, 2001), 1–2. Another collection of essays – Andrew Valls (ed.), *Race and Racism in Modern Philosophy* (Ithaca, NY: Cornell University Press, 2005) – is primarily concerned with establishing whether various eminent philosophers were racists. A related study is fatally limited by its concentration on practical knowledge and the contemporary US ordinary language idea of race: Joshua Glasgow, *A Theory of Race* (New York: Routledge, 2009).

18. Michael O. Hardimon, 'The Ordinary Concept of Race', *The Journal of Philosophy* 2003 100(9): 437–455, maintains that 'the ordinary concept of race and the ordinary conception of race are two different things' and presents what he regards as 'the concept's logical core' (439, 442). To the contrary, this book contends that practical knowledge about race has no logical core. Different strands within it may have historical cores.

19. Étienne Balibar and Immanuel Wallerstein, *Race, Nation, Class: Ambiguous Identities* (London: Verso, 1991), 37–67.

20. Stuart Hall, 'Race, articulation and societies structured in dominance', in *Sociological Theories: Race and Colonialism* (Paris: UNESCO, 1980), 331. Robert Miles, *Racism* (London: Routledge, 1989), 65, 84. Hall observes that 'one cannot explain racism in abstraction from other social relations' (337) – a clear statement of racism as explanandum. In this book, to the contrary, explanation is regarded as a process of deduction. Historical sequences may be interpreted, but not explained; interpersonal relations are usually multidimensional, and it is necessary to abstract an explanandum from them.

21. Robert Miles, *Racism and Migrant Labour* (London: Routledge, 1982), 31.

22. Miles, *Racism*, 84. The first use of 'racialization' in English was in 1977, when it was held that 'there was a social process, which can be called racialization, whereby a mode of classification was developed, applied tentatively in European historical writing, and then, more confidently, to the populations of the world'; see Michael Banton, *The Idea of Race* (London: Tavistock, 1977), 18–19. See also Karim Murji and John Solomos (eds.), *Racialization: Studies in Theory and Practice* (Oxford: Oxford University Press, 2005). Miles has

said 'there is no question that I "hijacked"' [Banton's] concept of racializa-tion' – Stephen D. Ashe and Brendan F. McGeever, 'Marxism, racism and the construction of "race" as a social and political relation: An interview with Professor Robert Miles', *Ethnic and Racial Studies* 2009 34(12): 2009–2026, at 2011.

23. Robert Miles and Malcolm Brown, *Racism*, 2nd edition (London: Rout-ledge, 2003), 96–99. Some contemporary authors fail to establish functional equivalence when they extend their use of 'racialization' to circumstances in which there has been no use of any racial idiom. Others write loosely of 'racism' in the plural, showing no awareness of the conceptual difficulties.

24. Kwame Anthony Appiah, *In My Father's House: Africa in the Philosophy of Culture* (London: Methuen, 1992), 18–19.

25. Pierre-André Taguieff, *Le racisme* (Paris: Flammarion, 1997), 11, 115–116. Tsvetan Tororov, 'Race and Racism', in Les Back and John Solomos (eds.), *Theories of Race and Racism* (London: Routledge, 2000), 64–70, at 64.

26. Joe R. Feagin, *Racist America: Roots, Current Realities, and Future Repara-tions*, 2nd edition (New York: Routledge, 2010), 11.

27. Michael Omi and Howard Winant, *Racial Formation in the United States: From the 1960s to the 1990s*, 2nd edition (New York: Routledge, 1994), 69–76.

28. Howard Winant, 'Racism today: A perspective from international politics', *Ethnic and Racial Studies* 1998 21(4): 765.

29. Eduardo Bonilla-Silva, 'Rethinking Racism: Toward a Structural Interpreta-tion', *American Sociological Review* 1996 62(3): 474.

30. David Theo Goldberg (ed.), *Anatomy of Racism* (Minneapolis: University of Minnesota Press, 1990), xiii.

31. Ali Rattansi, *Racism: A Very Short Introduction* (Oxford: Oxford University Press, 2007), 2.

32. Philomena Essed, 'Everyday Racism: A New Approach to the Study of Rac-ism', in Philomena Essed and David Theo Goldberg (eds.), *Race Critical The-ories: Text and Context* (Malden, MA: Blackwell, 2002), 176–194, esp. 177, 181.

33. Steve Garner, *Racisms: An Introduction* (Los Angeles: Sage, 2010).

34. Essed and Goldberg (eds.), *Race Critical Theories*, 4.

35. Stuart Hall, 'Cultural Studies and its Theoretical Legacies', in Nelson Gross-beg, Cary Lawrence and Paulo A. Treichler (eds.), *Cultural Studies* (New York: Routledge, 1992).

36. Pierre L. van den Berghe, 'Racism', in David Levinson and Melvin Ember (eds.), *Encyclopedia of Cultural Anthropology* (New York: Henry Holt & Co., 1996), 1054–1055.

Ethnic Origin and Ethnicity

In the United States, from the end of the nineteenth century, citizens of German and Irish origin were sometimes disparaged as 'hyphenated Americans'. It was alleged that they hesitated to become '100 per cent' Americans because they still clung to other 'loyalties'. 'Ethnic group' seems to have come into popular use as a more acceptable name for 'hyphenated Americans'.

In *The Social Systems of American Ethnic Groups*, written by W. Lloyd Warner and Leo Srole and published in 1945, the expression 'ethnic group' was used to designate eight cultural minorities of white 'race', resident in Massachusetts, who were on their way to becoming 'one hundred per cent Americans'.[1] The authors made no mention of 'ethnicity'; the first recorded use of that word is dated from 1953, when the sociologist David Riesman referred to 'the groups who, by reason of rural or small-town location, ethnicity, or other parochialism, feel threatened by the better educated upper-middle-class people'.[2]

Whether or not he intended this, Riesman's change from the adjective 'ethnic' to the noun 'ethnicity' implied that there was some distinctive quality in the sharing of a common ethnic origin that explained why people such as those he referred to might feel threatened by upper-middle-class people, who, apparently, did not attach the same significance to their own ethnic origins. They did not count as 'ethnics'.

Census Categories

In the English-speaking world, popular conceptions of 'race' and 'ethnicity' have been powerfully influenced by the requirements of governments when they carry out population censuses, issue passports and visas and compile official records. US censuses have, from the beginning, employed racial classifications. Starting with the 1910 census, a residual 'Other' category was provided, but the enumerators were instructed to enter the person's 'race' based on observation.[3] Much later, in 1975, the Office of Management and Budget made reference to 'Ethnicity' as a basis for classifying persons of Hispanic origin in order to monitor compliance with requirements for 'affirmative action'.

After two years, this circular (A-46), was revised to state that if separate race and ethnic categories were used, the minimum designations were:

a. Race:
☐ American Indian or Alaskan Native
☐ Asian or Pacific Islander
☐ Black
☐ White
b. Ethnicity:
☐ Hispanic origin
☐ Not of Hispanic origin

In the United Kingdom's census of 1991, residents in England and Wales were required to tick a box to indicate their ethnic group. They were offered seven possibilities: 'White, Black-Caribbean, Black-African, Black-Other (please describe), Indian, Pakistani, Bangladeshi, Chinese, Any other ethnic group (please describe)', and advised, 'If the person is descended from more than one ethnic or racial group, please tick the box to which the person considers he/she belongs, or tick the "Any other ethnic group" box and describe the person's ancestry in the space provided.'

There would have been vehement protests had any more general use been made of the word 'racial'. As already noted in the introduction, people may be ready to identify themselves with an ethnic group in a census because they understand why they are asked to do so, but they may not identify themselves with that ethnic group in any other circumstances. Initially, there were objections to the introduction of an ethnic question in the UK census, and to the recording of ethnic group when compiling statistics of employment and social housing. What was in question was the nature of an ethnic category and the implications of its recognition. Such a category is not necessarily a social group in practice.

In the United States, the relation between the Hispanic/Non-Hispanic distinction and the official conception of ethnicity is often obscure. Other countries use the category 'ethnic group' in whatever way suits them. Whereas in the United States 'ethnic group' became a subdivision of race, the government of Sweden chose to legislate against ethnic discrimination in employment; beliefs about 'racial' differences might be a ground of that discrimination, or of incitement to public disorder, but there was no recognition of any kind of racial group. In China, sixty-six ethnic groups are recognized. The census of 2010 recorded 1,220,844,520 persons as members of the Han group. The next largest was that of the Zhuang, with 16,926,381. The smallest was that of the Tatar, with 3,556 persons. The Han category was thus nearly twice as numerous as the population of Europe and was nearly four times that of the United States. Persons outside China must wonder about the value of such a large category if it is not subdivided.

For internal or constitutional reasons some states are opposed to the collection of ethnic statistics. Countries founded upon immigration, like Australia and Canada, have been more ready to recognize ethnic differences than European countries that until recently have been more accustomed to emigration. The constitution of France is built on a conception of the republic that will recognize no intermediary between the citizen and the state. No minorities, whether indigenous like the Bretons or the Corsicans, or immigrants like those of North African origin, can be recognized in France. As earlier noted, some African and other states consider it inadvisable to collect ethnic statistics for fear that the figures might exacerbate internal tensions.

Official practice has not been the only source of ethnic categorization. As Europeans explored other world regions and described the peoples they encountered, they often reported the names by which distinctive peoples identified themselves or were identified by others. In Africa they often categorized such groups as 'tribes'. For English speakers, this usage may have had origins in the King James Bible, with its references to 'the tribe of Benjamin' and the like. Since they did not speak of tribes within European countries, some Africans found use of this word disparaging; this might have encouraged the adoption of 'ethnic group' in place of tribe.

In the US census of 2010, 2.9 per cent of the total population indicated that they had origins in two or more races, an increase of 32 per cent over the figure recorded ten years earlier. Presumably these respondents wished to reject any implication that only one of their ethnic origins merited recognition. Given what is known about the distribution of genetic characteristics, it is certain that a far larger percentage of the population could, had they wished, have assigned themselves to the two-or-more category. More may do so as they become accustomed to the availability of this option.

Since many of the Americans with genetic origins in more than one world region will have identified themselves as 'black' in the census, it is within this category that changing identification is most to be expected. The political advantages brought in the 1960s by the polarization of the black and white categories may have declined, while it is also possible that many more people may wish to register their rejection of this kind of categorization. Among those who prefer to be identified as of mixed ancestry, many favour the expression 'multiracial'. This still retains a use of the racial idiom.

As mentioned in the introduction, many persons in the United States with multiple ethnic origins have, in the past, found that they could not get others to recognize them as neither black nor white. No third option was available to them. Now there is one. Answering the census question is a mode of self-identification with a community. In sociology it harks back to German notions of *Gemeinschaft*, and to Max Weber's questions about how a belief in shared origins can stimulate individuals to engage in collective action.

Anthropology

In the English language, the adjective 'ethnic' came into use initially to identify a certain kind of social group or category and as an improvement on some questionable uses of the word 'race'. It aided the growth of practical knowledge. One stimulus was a book of 1935 that was designed to explain to a popular readership how in Nazi Germany a kind of racial theory with pre-Darwinian origins was being used in a scientifically unjustifiable manner. Julian Huxley and A. C. Haddon maintained that 'ethnic group' would be a better name for the physical categories that bore names like Slav, Mediterranean, Nordic and Alpine; they thought it should replace the word 'race'.[4] As has also been noted earlier, fifteen years later an expert committee convened by UNESCO advised that 'it would be better when speaking of human races to drop the term "race" altogether and speak of ethnic groups'.[5] Both these conceptions were of an ethnic group as a population category independent of nations, states and their boundaries. They were intended as corrections of doctrines that claimed to be scientific.

In social and cultural anthropology it was customary to use 'ethnic group' as identifying a distinctive people with a common culture evident in their shared history, language and other characteristics. It was a practical classification, not one that presumed that all groups so designated shared a common quality of 'ethnicity'. That ethnic groups existed was not thought to pose any anthropological problem.

This changed after the publication in 1969 of *Ethnic Groups and Boundaries*. In its introduction, the Norwegian anthropologist Fredrik Barth maintained that the existence of an ethnic group depended not upon 'the cultural stuff' that its boundaries enclosed, but upon its ability to maintain those boundaries 'despite a flow of personnel' across them.[6] Contrary to the prevailing assumption, Barth contended that the existence of ethnic groups did constitute an anthropological problem. Thereafter, while 'ethnic group' continued in use as a practical classifier, it also became a kind of concept, though whether it has become a truly etic construct is uncertain. Barth inspired others to study the processes by which ethnic groups were created, maintained and sometimes dissolved. He had identified interesting new explananda.

Since then, social scientists have asked how ethnic boundaries came about, what work went into their maintenance and how they might be changed. Though he was not primarily concerned with ethnic groups as minorities, and their relations with states and with other minorities, Barth's arguments were extended to these fields. They were valuable in countering deterministic assumptions, in emphasizing the social construction of categories and in highlighting the views, intentions and self-perceptions of individual actors.[8] They helped in the formulation of better research questions. These were not necessarily questions about groups that had their own territory. For example, an author writing from Canadian experience commented on how urban life could offer scope for particular groups to monopolize occupational niches in the urban economy, and how shared ethnic origin could be a resource helping individuals to enter the marketplace.[7]

Barth discussed what he called 'identity change' with reference to four cases.[8] One was that of the Yao people on the southern fringe of the Chinese region. The Yao population was increasing by 10 per cent per annum because people from neighbouring groups were adopting Yao farming practices, securing adoption into Yao kin groups and undergoing ritual assimilation. The second example was of Pathans in Afghanistan who became Baluch, while the third came from the Sudan, where members of the Fur group of hoe agriculturalists were adopting the nomadic cattle-herding life of the Baggara, an Arab people.

The fourth example related to people of Lapp origin in northern Norway, some of whom were (and are) engaged in farming and fishing. They have changed in that their indigenous name, Saami, now has public recognition, and they are changing further by their adoption of many of the values of the Norwegian ethnic majority (for example, in claiming knowledge of other parts of Norway and in taking pride in well-furnished kitchens). Only in private did they speak in Saami, as if in public settings their ethnic identification constituted a stigma. In Barth's terms, they were on their way to assimilation because of the choices they were making. They were choosing the alternatives that, presumably, brought them the greater net benefits.

In African cities where newcomers from different ethnic groups encounter one another and speak a lingua franca, such changes in ethnic boundaries are common. There is a general tendency for ethnic origins to be ranked according to their associated degrees of socio-economic status, and sometimes for their dutifulness in fulfilling religious obligations. A person from a low-ranking group may conceal his or her origins, just as happens in modern industrial societies. A person may try to pass as a member of a favoured ethnic group if he or she stands to gain thereby.[9] Even if the person in question is not conscious of making any calculation of predicted costs and benefits, this supposition may offer a persuasive explanation of 'passing'. It would be in line with the view of social behaviour as exchange, or transactionalism, that Barth pioneered in some of his earlier work. Any conception of a scale of socio-economic status is founded upon the assumption that social attributes can be compared and that social behaviour will reflect a trade-off between possible gains and losses.

With the approach of self-government, ethnic categories in colonial territories acquired a new significance. 'Nationalist' leaders acted as political entrepreneurs; they advanced their views of the new alternatives that were being opened and recruited supporters. They could recruit most effectively by appealing for support on the basis of shared ethnic origin. They manufactured ethnic consciousness.[10]

This perspective can be employed in the study of the political changes in North America that followed the US Civil Rights movement, and the student activism of 1968. Quite apart from assertions of a 'right to be different', they stimulated a wave of 'identity politics' driven by the feminist, gay and lesbian liberation movements in association with demands for recognition made on behalf of ethnic minorities. The latter contributed to the pressure for courses on 'ethnic studies' in US universities that expressed the growing self-awareness and radicalization of people of color, such as African Americans, Asian Americans, Latino Americans and American Indians.

In Canada there was a new demand from French Canadians for the constitutional protection of their distinctiveness. In response, the Royal Commission on Bilingualism and Biculturalism recommended support for the cultural contributions of minority groups. From 1971, the expression 'multiculturalism' was introduced in Canada as a name for official programmes of cultural maintenance. It was then transplanted to Australia. In Britain it was first used to designate an educational philosophy alternative to that of anti-racism.

Words ending in '-ism' can accommodate many meanings, and so it was with multiculturalism. In an influential commentary on *Multiculturalism and 'The Politics of Recognition'*, Charles Taylor traced the new demands to conceptions of 'identity' as something known subjectively that summed up fundamental features of social being. He said, 'The thesis is that our identity is partly shaped by recognition or its absence', and that for lack of recognition, a person or group can suffer real damage.[11]

The demand for recognition was a political claim requiring a political response, but the word 'identity' can also be used as a concept in social science. From a policy standpoint, it might be useful to have some measures of the importance of this identity relative to the other identities or priorities of the claimants (quite apart from any consideration of evidence from genetic tests). From a social science standpoint, the concept of identity may have suffered overuse. Thus one important review concluded.

> Throughout this book, we have asked what work the concept is supposed to do, and how well it does it. We have argued that the concept is deployed to do a great deal of analytical work – much of it legitimate and important. 'Identity', however, is ill suited to perform this work, for it is riddled with ambiguity, riven with contradictory meanings and encumbered by reifying connotations.[12]

Many of these ambiguities arose from failures to specify sufficiently sharply the explananda that were being addressed.

A New Reality?

Reference to 'ethnic groups' was soon generalized by observations about 'ethnicity'. A volume edited by Nathan Glazer and Daniel Moynihan, *Ethnicity: Theory and Experience*, was very influential. It stemmed from a conference that had assembled theoretical and empirical studies of 'situations in which ethnic groups distinguish themselves'. The chief thrust, however, appears to have been the editors' concern with the emic construct of 'ethnicity' as an explanandum. They wrote: 'We are suggesting that a new word reflects a new reality and a new usage reflects a change in that reality. The new word is "ethnicity".'[13] Such a formulation takes the reader back to Weber's doubts about what this quality might be.

Many of the contributors provided analyses of particular situations that could be explicated by reference simply to ethnic groups and ethnic boundaries; one of them concluded that the 'term "ethnicity" is clearly a confusing one'.[14] Nevertheless, the editors' insisted that 'ethnicity' was 'a new reality'; they used the word as the title for the book; their encouragement of the view that the appearance on the political stage of 'ethnicity' was to be explained as the product of either primordialism or circumstantialism caught the attention of students of these matters. This formulation guided the course of teaching and research for a quarter-century.

At the time, Glazer and Moynihan's argument appeared to be a significant and original contribution to sociological knowledge. In retrospect it appears that their influence was, at least in part, negative. The reality that concerned them most was that members of the public, particularly in the United States, were displaying a heightened appreciation of their ethnic origins and were using shared ethnic origin as a basis for mobilization. European immigrants to that country had initially associated with their co-nationals. Later, when they realized that they would not return to live in their countries of origin, their co-nationals became their co-ethnics. The nature of the bond between the settlers had changed. Subsequent discussion centred upon the editors' question about the source of ethnicity: was it a primordial disposition, or was it a response to circumstances? Most commentators accepted that there was a thing, and that it was correctly identified. They concentrated on its outcome.

The Glazer and Moynihan volume, and the subsequent discussion, would have been different had the objective been to account for the significance that individuals attributed to their own and others' ethnic origin in given circumstances. This would have introduced a variable that is not measured when individuals specify an ethnic origin: When is ethnic origin socially relevant? Because they have no measure of within-category variation, those who use official statistics sometimes assume that most members of such a category will behave similarly. Measures of within-category variation are important to the assessment of social change.

The only contributor to query the relation of ethnic origin to national origin (and then only obliquely) was the demographer William Petersen. He wrote:

> What is lacking is a term similar in meaning to the European concept of a nation but applicable to a smaller population – that is, a people, a folk, held together by some or all of such more or less immutable characteristics as common descent, territory, history, language, religion, way of life, or other attributes that members of a group have from birth onward. In earlier writings, I have proposed the term subnation for these units.[15]

A subnation, in Petersen's sense, was a national minority that did not seek separation from the state within which its members were citizens. Had Glazer and Moynihan used subnation as the name for a set of individuals who wanted recognition of their distinctive character associated with their origin, and who might, in some circumstances, want a measure of autonomy, the subsequent course of discussion might have taken another direction.

Insofar as this argument held, the conference had to deal with an old reality, not a new one. It should have established stronger connections with scholarly writing about nationalism.

Nomenclature

Once a particular name for a category has become accepted it is easier to modify it than to challenge the original, probably unthinking, decision. The name 'race relations' now gives way to modifications like 'ethnic and racial relations'. With this in mind, it can be instructive to return to the conference that led to the 1955 book, *Race Relations in World Perspective*, discussed in chapter 4.

At that time the number one country for the study of race relations was the United States. That was where a theoretical framework had been developed. The number two country was South Africa. An Institute of Race Relations had been established in Johannesburg in 1929. There was on-going research. Two contributors to the World Perspective conference had agreed to contribute essays on the historical precedents and the more recent developments in South Africa; while both of them used the expression 'race relations' in their titles, they made scant use of it in the essays themselves.[16] The contributor who wrote on the history noted, 'When people in South Africa talk of "the two races", they often mean not Black and White, but the Afrikaans-speaking Whites and the English-speaking Whites. For, like the Bantu, the whites have been divided into rival national groups.' Writing on the currently prevailing situation, the other contributor began with the observation that, in deciding policy, the Whites 'have altogether over-looked the fact that there are other ethnic groups in the Union'.

Seen from a twenty-first-century standpoint, both authors could have laid aside the idiom of race and written about ethnic groups or subnations. In their generation this would have been difficult because the field of study had been defined as the study of race relations, and there was no conceptual framework for the study of ethnic relations.

At the time of the World Perspective conference, the political situation in South Africa was changing because the National Party government was implementing its plan for apartheid. The preeminent exponent of the plan's underlying philosophy was Hendrik Verwoerd, a social scientist who had been professor of Applied Sociology and Social Work at the University of Stellenbosch from 1932 to 1937 before he entered politics. He became prime minister in 1958, and served in this position until his assassination eight years later.

From his days as a schoolboy, Verwoerd was preoccupied with what he perceived as the problem of white poverty; he saw this from the perspective of an Afrikaner nationalist. In his sociology lectures, Verwoerd presented an evolutionist perspective taking the form of cultural-historical theory in which black South Africans were part of a completely different civilization. Biological determinism and racial theory played only insignificant parts in his argument. The nature of a people, a *volk*, was the key element. A careful study of his philosophy has concluded: 'The fact that Verwoerd saw whites and blacks as belonging to different cultures was not in itself racist, but his perception of each as captive to these cultures was.'[17]

It seems clear that the names 'ethnic group' and 'nationalism' better represent social categories and sentiment in South Africa both before and after the end of apartheid than the nomenclature used at the World Perspective conference. Indeed, it can be argued, with the benefit of hindsight, that the conference itself might well have been on Ethnic Relations in World Perspective. Someone might have maintained that during the nineteenth century, African Americans became an ethnic group. The idiom of race had a place in the study of white attitudes and behaviour, not in the study of the black response to this behaviour. It could have inspired a little book on the strange career of Jim Crow's creator, the new white ideology and its institutional expression.

A movement to reassess use of the idiom of race could have started in the 1950s, but any attempt to replace it with an idiom of ethnicity would have had to relate ethnic sentiment to national sentiment. There was, and still is, no agreement about how the word 'nationalism' is best employed or how it should relate to ethnicity.

The extent of the disagreement may be illustrated by recalling the declaration of a critic of nationalist claims when he asserted, 'Nationalism is a doctrine invented in Europe at the beginning of the nineteenth century. It pretends to supply a criterion for the determination of the unit of population proper to enjoy a government exclusively its own, for the legitimate exercise of power in the state, and for the right organization of a society of states.'[18] This expressed what has been considered an idealist theory of nationalism, making national sentiment a cause of political action and not a result of it. The Eurocentric orientation of that theory has been counterbalanced by the thesis that nations are 'imagined communities' and that the sentiment has sources in the cultures of non-European peoples as well.[19]

A radically different diagnosis of the origins of national sentiment was advanced by Ernest Gellner; he portrayed the nation-state as a product of modernity. Gellner's account was opposed in turn by Anthony Smith who emphasized the ethnic origins of nations. The challenge sparked a lively debate.[20]

Each nation is unique, but forms of government can be classified. Earlier, Hans Kohn had contended that some European states, notably Germany, were founded upon an ethnic conception of the nation, whereas other states, notably France, subordinated notions of a national bond to a doctrine that the state and the citizen were bound by a civic bond.[21] Ethnic nationalism was presented as undemocratic and irrational, civic nationalism as rational and democratic.

In the United States, hyphenate groups could be accounted ethnic; it was a practical way of making sense of the general situation. Likewise, groups in Europe could be accounted ethnic because of the association between the ethnic and the national. This is not a universal association. The hyphenate usage was not acceptable to some French Canadians (or *Québéçois*), because of their insistence that they are a nation, not a subdivision of a state that fails fully to recognize their distinctiveness. One writer objects that 'by using the term ethnic, one is perceived as negating the legitimate right of a national community to self-determination.'[22] A similar argument underlies the position adopted by those African Americans who are known as black nationalists.

In sociology, support has grown for the argument that it is unwise to examine racial distinctions in isolation from ethnic distinctions, or to study ethnic distinctions apart from national distinctions. This was acknowledged when the editors of the *Annual Review of Sociology* for 2009 commissioned a review of sociological writing about 'ethnicity, race and nationalism'.[23]

The philosophical problems arose with the use of 'ethnicity' as a noun, not with its use as an adjective, as in 'ethnic group' and 'ethnic origin'. To write of 'ethnicity', as Glazer and Moynihan did, was to represent ethnicity as a thing, to reify it. The reality is that individuals vest ethnic origin with social significance. There are variables here that have not yet been examined systematically.

The US population can now be described as including five panethnic categories, African American, Asian American, European American, Hispanic American and Native American.[24] In some circumstances, new names are needed to differentiate those African Americans and European Americans whose ancestors came to the United States before and after the Civil War from African Americans and Europeans whose origins in the United States are more recent. Some persons, such as Hispanic Americans of European descent, may be able to claim places in more than one panethnic category.

Sociobiology

If ethnic identification was to be seen as 'a new reality', it was one that depended upon the construction that individuals put upon their social circumstances. This might not be the end of the matter. Pierre L. van den Berghe maintained in 1981 that ethnicity was an extension of kinship, and that the significance attributed to kinship enabled humans to maximize inclusive fitness in their struggle for a biological future. Social behaviour had a biological foundation. His model then assumed that people behave cooperatively with others to the extent that they share interests, or believe that they do, or that they are co-erced into behaving in ways contrary to their interests (in which case they are forced to play the game of minimizing loss rather than max-imizing gain).[25]

This thesis has been supported by findings reported from studies of social associations with variations in skin colour. These variations have been measured with spectrometers in thirty-two groups living in every major world region. The results show that sexual selection has been in operation. A lighter complexion increases a woman's opportu-nities for marriage, as if men, perhaps unconsciously, 'choose women more on the basis of physical characteristics (such as youth, health and body fat) that are linked to reproductive value, while women tend to select men on the basis of male readiness and capacity to invest re-sources in raising their offspring'. These differences can be accounted for as the outcome of 'a genetically based sexual dimorphism in skin pigmentation'. On the larger scale, they support the conclusion that, to persist, human culture must 'serve the reproductive interests of its flesh and blood carriers'.[26]

The evidence that men and women choose partners on the basis of different characteristics and place a different value upon pigmentation is highly relevant to sociological research, but few sociologists have the technical competence to assess the claim that the sexual dimor-phism serves a biological interest. This issue brings up the philosophi-cal difficulties that centre upon the nature of sociological explanation. The view urged here is that the sociologist's task is to assess whether a perception of a particular shade of skin colour can help account for an observation about observed behaviour.

Ethnic Origin as a Social Sign

Any attempt to account for the significance that individuals attribute to their own and others' ethnic origin in given circumstances can well start from the proposition (mentioned earlier) that when two persons meet, either one of them may perceive something about the other that suggests that he or she has a distinctive ethnic or national origin. In Yankee City, as represented by Lloyd Warner, a Yankee might perceive someone as Irish-American or Italian-American, subdivisions of what Warner considered a racial category. The same person might perceive another person as Puerto Rican, an ethnic subdivision of the black category, or as Canadian, assigning him or her to a national category. In Marseilles, a French person might perceive another as Corsican or Basque or as Italian, assigning the first two to ethnic categories, and the third person to a national category. In London, a man in a kilt might be assigned to a national category – as a Scot – but to a national category of a kind different from the national category to which an Italian would be assigned, because the United Kingdom can be considered a multinational state. In the East End of London, a man with brown skin, a particular kind of white cap and a long gown might be assigned to a national category, as Bangladeshi, to a religious category, as Muslim, or to an ethnic category, as a Briton of Bangladeshi origin. In chapter 4, Maurice Freedman was quoted as observing, 'In the study of race relations the student has crossed his pons asinorum when he has learned to define his "races" afresh for each new situation he is called upon to discuss.' The same principle applies to use of the notion of ethnicity.

The social significance of a sign of minority ethnic origin varies with the kind of ethnic or national majority. In the United States, where everyone is of immigrant origin except persons of Native American descent, a sign of ethnic origin is not necessarily an indicator of recent immigration. In countries like Malaysia, in which members of one group regard themselves as a *Staatsvolk*, a sign of non-majority ethnic origin indicates someone who is not entitled to *Staatsvolk* privileges. In Malaysia, as in many countries, a person of minority ethnic origin may be at a disadvantage even though he or she is a citizen.

Sociological research has also described a related kind of situation. In parts of Romania that used to be parts of Hungary, use of the Hungarian language may rouse Romanian suspicions that the persons in question are not behaving as Romanians should.[27] When members of a minority ethnic group want to be part of a different state, signs of their ethnic origin raise issues of interstate relations. For sociological analysis, the significance of ethnic origin in situations that raise questions of interstate relations may need to be treated separately from interethnic relations within states. (Note that here, as elsewhere in this book, 'state' refers to the US federal state, not to its constituent components.)

In the United States, however, much sociological research has been directed towards the country's public policy concerns. Prominent among them has been the settlement and assimilation of immigrants and migrant workers from Mexico and other Latin American countries. Research into diaspora processes and into conceptions of identity has sometimes overlapped with this. In general, though, research publications refer mostly to closely related studies without much sense of connection to general and comparative work. This is consistent with the doubts about any claim that racial and ethnic studies constitute a properly conceptualized subfield within the social sciences.

Comparative Politics

At the beginning of chapter 4 it was claimed that psychology was the first of the social sciences to build theoretical knowledge about social interaction in general, including black-white interaction, without being dependent upon any concept of race. Economics came next. Sociologists have struggled with the problem for a century, but now, with the creation of comparative politics as a recognized division of political science, they have the support of new and powerful allies. Students of comparative politics bring special skills, such as those needed to make good use of the theory of games, described by Jon Elster as probably 'the most important single advance of the social sciences in the twentieth century'.[28]

The book that best represents this new development is Donald L. Horowitz's *Ethnic Groups in Conflict* of 1985; it made a major contribution to practical knowledge. Horowitz aimed to set out an understanding of the nature of ethnic affiliations, and an explanation of ethnic conflict with a primary focus on severely divided societies in Africa and Asia. The author's approach was 'to get the hands dirty, in the double sense of dealing with the often seamy side of ethnic politics and of looking closely at the details of actual cases'. In particular, he asked what it is about ethnic affiliations that makes them conducive to severe conflict?

The conception of ethnicity he employed did not separate 'race' from 'ethnicity', but embraced 'differences identified by color, language, religion, or some other attribute of common origin' and treated ethnicity as 'functionally continuous with kinship'.[29] The primary concern was with the influence of ethnic affiliation upon state politics, recognizing that ethnic affiliation was not unitary but might include 'subethnic division'. Ethnicity was therefore treated as an explanandum rather than as an explanans, and the conflicts considered were those between mobilized groups. It did not directly discuss variations in the significance attributed to differences of ethnic origin.

While this may well be the best way to advance an 'understanding' of the phenomena in question, no explanation of ethnic conflict can be complete if it does not explain why there can be situations of ethnic contact without conflict, and that ethnic differences do not necessarily lead to collective action by both parties. Any vision of conflict as a group phenomenon is likely to rely on the oversocialized conception of the actor, as a person who always conforms to group expectations.

The strength of *Ethnic Groups in Conflict* lies, as promised, in the analysis of ethnic politics, of the circumstances that inspire military coups and of political measures designed to reduce the likelihood of coups or of secessions. A particular strength of Horowitz's contribution is his exposition of 'constitutional engineering', the possibilities, for example, of reducing conflict within federal states by increasing the number of units that constitute the federation, or by revising their boundaries, by devolution, by preferential policies or by changing the electoral system. For example, under the constitution of Nigeria as it was in 1979, to be elected president a candidate had to secure at least 25 per cent of the vote in two-thirds of the federation's states.[30] This discouraged candidates from trying to pile up votes by appealing to ethnic constituencies.

Research in comparative politics holds out a possibility of bringing an analysis of state and national institutions into the same conceptual framework as the analysis of racial and ethnic relations. A test case is presented by studies of intergroup conflict in India, where distinctions of belief and descent are drawn in ways that parallel distinctions of racial and ethnic origin. There are also puzzling variations, since there is violent conflict between Hindus and Muslims in some cities but not in others. Ashutosh Varshney wondered why eight cities, containing just 18 per cent of India's population, should have accounted for nearly half of the total deaths from Hindu-Muslim urban violence between 1950 and 1995. So he compared the conflict-prone city of Aligarh with the relatively conflict-free city of Calicut.[31] In both cities there were oppositions between Hindus and Muslims, and in both cities committees to prevent violence had been established. They were effective in Calicut because of the counterbalancing effect of caste divisions among the Hindus and because the interest of the local political elite lay in the prevention of violence. In Aligarh, by contrast, different sections of the elite could gain from Hindu-Muslim conflict.

This study took violence as a criterion for determining when an opposition became a conflict, which would be an undue limitation in the study of some of the conflicts regarded as racial or ethnic. A more general question was raised by Varshney's readiness to count Hindu-Muslim violence as ethnic conflict (rather than religious conflict). An Indian sociologist, discussing other political conflicts in the Indian subcontinent, has similarly presented them as instances of 'coping with ethnicity'. There are genuine questions about how the Bangladeshis came to feel themselves a separate people, about why Sikh group consciousness has risen and fallen and about the nature of a Kashmiri identity, but calling them ethnic problems is only a redescription. It does not add to explanation of the processes in question.[32]

Some questions have a bottom-up character. Why is one category of persons attacked rather than another? After the assassination in 1984, by a Punjabi Sikh, of Prime Minister Indira Gandhi, mobs in Delhi attacked Sikhs, but those they attacked were Sikhs from parts of India other than the Punjab, and the victims were not supporters of Punjabi separatism. In the northern Nigerian town of Kano, in 1953 and again in 1966, Ibo settlers from southern regions were attacked, but not Yoruba settlers. The northerners had just as much reason to suspect the political and commercial ambitions of the Yoruba from the southwest as the Ibo from the southeast. Why should one group have been victimized while another remained unharmed?

Many Asian and African states have been challenged by minority movements seeking to secede. Bangladesh and South Sudan were successful. Biafra and many others have been unsuccessful. According to Horowitz, the emergence of such a movement is determined mainly by domestic politics, but whether it will succeed is determined largely by international politics. These issues have been taken further in a study of the policies of European states that have attempted, or might have attempted, to recover lost territory.[33] Why, for example, did Armenia in 1991 go to war with Azerbaijan in order to establish a corridor linking up with an Armenian enclave living in Azerbaijani territory? It proved an expensive venture, and the Armenian claim that they have revised their state borders has not been acceptable to other states.

Why did Croatia try to grab portions of Bosnia inhabited by fellow Croats, and Serbia risk so much on behalf of Serbs outside Serbia? If these actions are attributed to nationalism, why did not Hungary try to renegotiate its boundary with Romania to recover some of the territory it lost in 1920? Romania lost Bessarabia in 1939; it later became the independent state of Moldova. Why did not Romania and Moldova reunite after 1989? Why, after the dissolution of the USSR, was not more done to bring the twenty-five millions outside Russia into closer relation with their motherland?

Aggressive attempts to change borders in order to bring co-ethnics back into the nation-state are examples of irredentism. Though they raise practical issues central to the study of comparative politics, any attempt to explain them in theoretical terms as the product of ethnic solidarity raises difficulties of definition.[34] When the issue is one of interstate relations, is it not a matter of national rather than ethnic sentiment?

When, in 1916, the United States declared war on Germany, the change in circumstances forced German Americans to decide whether they were to be members of an ethnic minority loyal to the state in which they resided, or whether they were to be German nationals and accept the possibility that they would be interned for the duration of the war. For practical purposes, a distinction had to be drawn between an ethnic bond and a national bond. Whether there are theoretical purposes for drawing a parallel distinction is not yet certain. The formation of a nation-state is sometimes seen as an outcome of ethnic sentiment among persons who have been citizens of a different state. So long as they were agitating for union with their kin state, they would have been a national minority. If, on the other hand, the government of the state in which they found themselves gave them greater autonomy, secessionist sentiment might decline, and the persons in question might continue as members of an ethnic minority. Such a formulation can guide use of the adjectives 'ethnic' and 'national', but it does not provide a way of distinguishing between 'ethnicity' and 'nationalism' if these are thought to motivate behaviour.

Chapter 4 has already introduced the claimed existence of 'plural' societies as composed of ethnically and culturally distinctive social categories that do not actively seek to change any territorial borders. In a book titled *Politics in Plural Societies: A Theory of Democratic Instability*, Alvin Rabushka and Kenneth A. Shepsle brought the issue into comparative politics.[35] It was cited as the first example of the use of rational choice theory in the study of race and ethnic relations.[36] The authors noted developments in eighteen plural societies in Asia, Africa, South America, the Middle East, Europe and the Caribbean. Most were former colonies that became independent after World War II, but the coverage extended to others, including Belgium, South Africa, Yugoslavia, Lebanon and Northern Ireland. Rabushka and Shepsle elaborated a formal model of decision theory, featuring techniques for the analysis of decision taking. The techniques in question, however, were applicable in the analysis of all kinds of economy provided due account was taken of imperfect competition.[37]

Some authors have proposed the analysis of pluralism without claiming that there are distinctive plural societies. One table summarizing high, medium and low degrees of pluralism lists the number, relative size and geographical distribution of ethnic, racial or caste groups, the clarity and rigidity of their boundaries, together with the range of institutional autonomy, the multiplication, distinctiveness and compatibility of institutions, the degree, range and compatibility of values and the compatibility of membership in distinctive kinds of social networks.[38] Though the differences are real and relevant, that is not sufficient to make pluralism into an explanatory concept. The next chapter will argue that many of the divisions are better explained as the products of social closure by groups pursuing sectional interests.

As a further example of the kinds of contribution that can be expected from political scientists, reference may be made to David Laitin's investigations of the relative strength of different social identifications in promoting the coordination of social action. In a Somali school he set up a field experiment to test his hypothesis that use of the Somali language would promote a more egalitarian view of the relation between a headmaster and a class teacher than would use of the English language. The results confirmed his hypothesis. In Nigeria he hypothesized that Yoruba Christians would find authority in the Christian scriptures and Muslims in their imam's sermons. He found instead that Yoruba sought no political advantage by appealing to religious differences, but divided according to ancestral city origin. This had become the salient dimension of social relations in the southwest of the country, whereas religion had become the salient dimension in the north. Laitin's explanation was that individuals had collectively chosen the dimension that gave them the optimal political returns within the state's system of resource allocation.[39]

A sophisticated application of similar techniques was employed in an innovatory study conducted in Kampala, Uganda, by four political scientists.[40] Unlike previous studies, it measured the influence of ethnic identifications instead of deducing their influence from observation, and it produced new findings that went beyond the kind of information previously available. How much use was the concept of ethnicity for the elucidation of these findings?

Members of the public do not always act in accordance with what others believe to be their interests. The Kampala researchers reported that the residents of the poorer neighbourhoods of the town had to cope with major problems of drainage, garbage removal and personal security. Heavy rainfall caused severe flooding, and this was made more serious by the accumulation of refuse in the open drains. The city council failed to keep all the drains clear and to remove all the garbage. Community patrols had once served to deter criminal behaviour, but were no longer funded. The resulting constant threat of theft had reduced the quality of local life. Why then did the residents of many neighbourhoods not themselves organize to remove garbage and restore the community patrols by establishing a neighbourhood watch?

Several earlier studies had reported that cooperative action takes place more readily among socially homogeneous groups. While the Kampala study supported the conclusion that ethnically heterogeneous communities have greater difficulty acting collectively, the researchers concluded that the mere sharing of ethnic origin did not provide a sufficient explanation. They found that underlying the social behaviour they studied there appeared to be a universal norm of reciprocity. The subjects apparently found it easier to develop reciprocal relations with co-ethnics; that helped account for the initiation of collective action.

The researchers drew a random sample of three hundred residents in one neighbourhood. They checked to see if their subjects, given differing amounts of information, could identify other members of their sample ethnically (some could not); they then investigated whether subjects behaved differently in relations with those they believed to be co-ethnics. They differentiated 'benchmark demographics' (in which the subject correctly identified the other party with one of the ethnic categories employed by the Uganda Bureau of Statistics) and 'subjective demographics' (in which the subject identified the other party in some other way).

They showed subjects photographs of potential partners, offering them rewards if they identified co-ethnics. Then they added an indication of the language spoken by the other party and that person's given and family names to see how much this improved their identifications. They found that some persons and groups could not be easily identified. The findings suggested that the ethnic categories reflected only poorly the social categories that were used in everyday life (the subjective demographics). Sometimes regional origin was more important than ethnic or benchmark origin.

Earlier studies had reported that cooperative action takes place more readily along ethnic lines than across them, and that ethnically heterogeneous communities have greater difficulty acting collectively. To investigate the link between ethnic diversity and ability to cooperate in securing public goods, the researchers took a lead from the Prisoner's Dilemma game. In that game, both players benefit if they cooperate. If one contributes to collective action and the other does not, then the would-be cooperator becomes a 'sucker'. He or she gets little return on the investment, while the other party takes a 'free ride'. Cooperative action by one player alone is not fairly rewarded.

The three hundred subjects attended four sessions in which, motivated by the prospect of significant reward, they played a series of games designed to measure the significance of different possible determinants. Two of the general findings were that co-ethnics engaged more frequently with each other and were more likely to punish each other for failing to cooperate, but some of the detailed findings could not have been predicted in advance and they opened interesting questions for further research.

Other studies had shown that subjects vary in the degree to which they prioritize material gain for themselves. To allow for this, the Kampala subjects were divided into egoists and non-egoists. This was done by use of a version of the Dictator game in which subjects can decide how much of the reward they will distribute and how much they will keep for themselves. This indicated that an egoist was more likely to cooperate with the other player if that player was thought to be a co-ethnic. To find out if this came from an expectation of reciprocity, the researchers gave the players additional information about the identity of the other players. Removal of the condition of anonymity had a significant effect upon the behaviour of the egoists, but none on the non-egoists. The results showed that if co-ethnics cooperate more effectively in producing public goods, it is not simply because they value more highly the happiness of other group members, care about the same things or simply prefer working with co-ethnics. It is because perceived sharing of ethnic origin can generate strategies that promote cooperation. The subjects themselves recognized that the games they were invited to play mirrored their everyday problems.

If such findings can be confirmed, they will point to an unconscious source of ethnic preferences, one that could not easily have been found by any other research method. It could be the beginning of a progressive research programme. The theory of games opens avenues for the study of conditions favourable to the development of reciprocal relations.

While the authors acknowledged that the significance of 'ethnicity' was powerfully influenced by national politics, and were cautious about generalizing their findings, they did not sufficiently question either the nature of what is called ethnicity or what characterizes the circumstances in which a co-ethnic is considered a potential ally.

It looks as if, in Kampala, someone from the same region may be as good an ally as a co-ethnic, but by taking the classification employed by the Uganda Bureau of Statistics as their benchmark, the authors turned down the opportunity to learn more about the logic within the 'subjective demographics'. Nevertheless this path-breaking research demonstrated that, by tapping unconscious influences, the experimental study of ethnic preferences can contribute new knowledge.

The Current Sociology of Ethnicity

Student texts about ethnicity have not yet caught up with all these developments in research. Most authors take as their point of departure the ordinary language meaning of the word instead of trying to explain the behaviour that is designated by the word. Thus the author of *The Sociology of Ethnicity* focused on the meaning given to the word by fellow sociologists; he stated, 'Ethnicity is not a thing or a collective asset of a particular group; it is a social relation in which social actors perceive themselves and are perceived by others as being distinct collectivities.'[41] He presented 'ethnicity' as an explanandum rather than as an explanans.

The author of a second text perceived a problem of definition when he asked, 'How are we in principle to distinguish ethnic attachments from kinship, neighbourhood or organizational attachments, for example, and how, correspondingly, can we compare different "ethnic" situations?' His proposed solution did not consider whether the concept was fit for an accepted purpose. Nor did it address the differentiation of ethnic from national origin. It was to advance a model in which

> Ethnicity is a matter of cultural differentiation ...
> – centrally a matter of shared meanings ...
> – no more fixed or unchanging ...
> – as an identification, is collective and ... individualized in personal self-identification.[42]

This is to presume that there is a common element to all the instances in which 'ethnic attachments' are noted.

A third author discussed some of the related philosophical difficulties, but concluded that 'a theory of ethnicity has to be a theory of the contexts in which it is "activated"'. This was an unfortunate metaphor because it suggests that there is a general and distinctive sentiment properly so named.[43] Like other authors, he started from the name instead of from an observation. Yet with the worldwide increase in 'ethnic tourism', the words 'race' and 'ethnicity' are acquiring new meanings that emphasize the exotic.[44] The significance of a shared ethnic origin varies from place to place: it is not the same in the United States for hyphenates as it is for North American Indian groups whose special status enables them to open lucrative casino enterprises and to remake themselves in the image of the corporation.[45] It is not the same in Quebec as it is in the rest of Canada, or in the African countryside compared with the towns. If, as appears to be the case, there are no problems that can be solved only by using a concept of ethnicity, then ethnicity, like racism, is to be regarded as an emic construct. The social scientist has to look elsewhere for theoretical inspiration.

As has been argued from the beginning of this book, a better strategy is to start from an intellectual problem. This has been exemplified by a study of interpersonal relations in three urban neighbourhoods in Switzerland. The author, Andreas Wimmer, asked, 'Does ethnicity matter in processes of everyday group formation?' Without assuming that the residents formed groups based on ethnic origin, he collected information on ethnic origin as he did on other possibly relevant variables.[46] His results told him that 'ethnic-national groups

... do not play ... a central role ... in the social world of our informants. ... They did not divide themselves and others into groups based on ethnicity ... but in accordance with ... a central scheme of order.' In considering whether newly arrived residents were treated as 'outsiders', whether they helped keep the courtyard tidy and followed the rules of the building counted for more than their ethnic origin. Thus Wimmer's explanandum was everyday group formation in such neighbourhoods. His explanans was that acceptance reflected conformity to neighbourhood social norms. He has since developed this argument in ways that will be mentioned later.

If a new species of plant or animal is discovered, a description of a type specimen is published in a scientific journal and the type specimen is deposited in a natural history museum where, if necessary, it can be examined by other researchers. Sociologists have no type specimen of 'ethnicity', and cannot reliably differentiate ethnicity from other variables with which it is associated. Though this problem should have been identified after the publication of Glazer and Moynihan's influential volume *Ethnicity* in 1975, it has not yet been properly confronted.

The word 'ethnicity' has no agreed meaning in sociology. If the social sciences were more like botany, there might be greater agreement on how a people, a nation and an ethnic group are to be differentiated and defined. As it is, social science research workers do not address problems of a kind that obliges them to select the best performing concepts. Too many of the authors who have set out to discuss ethnicity – like those who have discussed racism – have started from a word instead of from an explanandum. They might have done better had they differentiated practical and theoretical knowledge. Further experimental research (not necessarily of the kind described here) offers the best hope that someday social scientists may be able to uncover regularities that underlie the expressions employed in ordinary language.

Notes

1. W. Lloyd Warner and Leo Srole, *The Social Systems of American Ethnic Groups* (New Haven: Yale University Press, 1945).
2. David Riesman, *American Scholar* 1953 XXIII(1): 15.
3. Sharon M. Lee, 'Racial Classifications in the US Census: 18901990', *Ethnic and Racial Studies* 1993 16(1): 75–94; Prewitt, *What is Your Race?* 135.

4. Julian Huxley and A. C. Haddon, *We Europeans: A Survey of Racial Problems* (London: Cape, 1935), 91–92.
5. UNESCO, *Four Statements on the Race Question* (Paris: UNESCO, 1969).
6. Fredrik Barth (ed.), *Ethnic Groups and Boundaries* (Oslo: Universitetsforlaget, 1969), 9, 15.
7. Sandra Wallman, 'The Scope for Ethnicity', in Wallman (ed.), *Ethnicity At Work* (London: Macmillan, 1979), 1–14.
8. Barth, *Ethnic Groups and Boundaries*, 22–24, 39–43.
9. The city of Freetown was founded in 1787 within the territory of the Temne ethnic group. A Temne leader who, on Sierra Leone's independence, became deputy prime minister, described the situation in the mid-1940s as follows: 'The Temnes in the City were moving rapidly wards detribalization, some becoming Creoles and others Akus and Mandingoes. The first were the educated ones in English and others who were not educated but have come to Freetown to seek jobs. The reason for the exodus from the Temne tribe was the backwardness of the Temnes socially and economically. To be considered favourably was to call yourself a Mandingo, Creole or Aku. This protective measure was adopted in many forms, dress, language and in joining foreign dances. Consequently every bright looking young Temne is lost to the other tribes and the word Temne is associated with the uncivilized people.' Michael Banton, *West African City: A Study of Tribal Life in Freetown* (London: Oxford University Press, 1957), 165.
10. Alvin Rabushka and Kenneth A. Shepsle, *Politics in Plural Societies: A Theory of Democratic Instability,* 2nd edition (New York: Pearson, 2009 [1972]), 59–61.
11. Charles Taylor, *Multiculturalism and 'The Politics of Recognition'*, (Princeton: Princeton University Press, 1992), 25. Although the dictionary already acknowledged the verb 'to miscognize', Taylor coined the expression 'misrecognition'. To recognize is to make a correct identification. An incorrect identification is a miscognition.
12. Rogers Brubaker and Frederick Cooper, 'Beyond Identity', *Theory and Society* 2000 29(1): 1–47, reprinted in Rogers Brubaker, *Ethnicity Without Groups* (Cambridge, MA: Harvard University Press, 2004), 28–63, at 61. Many of the arguments in this chapter run parallel with those in this book.
13. Nathan Glazer and Daniel Patrick Moynihan (eds.), *Ethnicity: Theory and Experience* (Cambridge MA: Harvard University Press, 1975).
14. Daniel Bell, 'Ethnicity and Social Change', in ibid., 141–174, at 156.
15. William Petersen, 'On the Subnations of Western Europe', in ibid., 177–208, at 181–182.
16. John A. Barnes, 'Race Relations in the Development of Southern Africa', and Absolom Vilakazi, 'Race Relations in South Africa', both in Andrew W. Lind (ed.), *Race Relations in World Perspective: Papers read at the Conference on Race Relations in World Perspective,* Honolulu, 1954 (Honolulu: University of Hawaii Press, 1955), 167–186 and 313–338.
17. Christoph Marx, 'Hendrik Verwoerd's Long March to Apartheid: Nationalism and Racism in South Africa', in Manfred Berg and Simon Wendt (eds.),

Racism in the Modern World: Historical Perspectives on Cultural Transfer and Adaptation (New York: Berghahn Books, 2011), 281–302, at 294.

18. Elie Kedourie, *Nationalism* (London: Hutchinson, 1960), 9.
19. Benedict Anderson, *Imagined Communities: Reflections of the Origin and Spread of Nationalism* (London: Verso, 1983).
20. *Nations and Nationalism* 1996 2(3) contains articles by Anthony D. Smith, 'Opening statement: Nations and their pasts', 357; Ernest Gellner, 'Reply: Do nations have navels?' 358–370; and Anthony D. Smith, 'Memory and Modernity: reflections on Ernest Gellner's theory of nationalism', 371–388.
21. Hans Kohn, *The Idea of Nationalism* (New York: Collier Books, 1944).
22. Danielle Juteau, 'Pures laines' Québécois: the concealed ethnicity of dominant minorities', in Eric P. Kaufman (ed.), *Rethinking Ethnicity: Majority Groups and Dominant Minorities* (London: Routledge, 2004), 84–101, at 98 note 14.
23. Rogers Brubaker, 'Ethnicity, Race and Nationalism', 2009 *Annual Review of Sociology* 2009 35: 21–42.
24. UK English-language speakers may wish to hyphenate Afro-Americans and Euro-Americans. For the United States, see Dina G. Okamoto, *Redefining Race: Asian American Panethnicity and Shifting Ethnic Boundaries* (New York: Russell Sage Foundation, 2014).
25. Pierre L. van den Berghe, *The Ethnic Phenomenon* (Amsterdam: Elsevier, 1981); 'Ethnicity and the sociobiology debate', in John Rex and David Mason (eds.), *Theories of Race and Ethnic Relations* (Cambridge: Cambridge University Press, 1986), 246–263.
26. Pierre L. van den Berghe and Peter Frost, 'Skin Colour Preference, Sexual Dimorphism and Sexual Selection: a case of gene culture co-evolution?' *Ethnic and Racial Studies* 1986 9(1): 87–113. See also Peter Frost, *Fair Women, Dark Men: The Forgotten Roots of Color Prejudice* (Christchurch: Cybereditions, 2005).
27. Rogers Brubaker et al., *Nationalist Politics and Everyday Ethnicity in a Transylvanian Town* (Princeton: Princeton University Press, 2006).
28. Jon Elster, *Explaining Social Behaviour: More Nuts and Bolts for the Social Sciences* (Cambridge: Cambridge University Press, 2007), 312.
29. Donald L. Horowitz, *Ethnic Groups in Conflict* (Berkeley: University of California Press, 2000 [1985]), 41, 78.
30. Ibid., 637. Horowitz's *A Democratic South Africa? Constitutional Engineering in a Divided Society* (Berkeley: California University Press, 1991) influenced the drafting of the post-1994 constitution of South Africa. It has been followed by *Constitutional Change and Democracy in Indonesia* (Cambridge: Cambridge University Press, 2013).
31. Ashutosh Varshney, *Ethnic Conflict and Civic Life: Hindus and Muslims in India* (New Haven: Yale University Press, 2002).
32. T. N. Madan, 'Coping with ethnicity in South Asia: Bangadesh, Punjab and Kashmir compared', *Ethnic and Racial Studies* 1989 21(5): 969–989; and Michael Banton, 'Are there ethnic groups in South Asia?' ibid. 21(5): 990–994.

33. Stephen Saidemann and R. William Ayres, *For Kin or Country: Xenophobia, Nationalism, and War* (New York: Colombia University Press, 2008).

34. For a theoretically sophisticated example of the analysis of political action regarding possible border revision in central Europe and the Balkans between 1938 and 1939, see Rein K. Jenne, *Ethnic Bargaining: The Paradox of Minority Empowerment* (New York: Cornell University Press, 2007).

35. Rabushka and Shepsle, *Politics in Plural Societies*.

36. Michael Hechter, 'Rational choice theory and the study of race and ethnic relations', in John Rex and David Mason (eds.), *Theories of Race and Ethnic Relations* (Cambridge: Cambridge University Press, 1986), 264–275.

37. Rabushka and Shepsle, *Politics in Plural Societies*, 66, characterize the plural society as one in which 'ethnic preferences are intense and are not negotiable'. The situation in Java in Furnival's day was supposed to be the classic example of a plural society, but the re-examination of the evidence by Coppel showed that the ethnic preferences there were negotiable.

38. van den Berghe, *Race and Racism*, 142–143.

39. See David D. Laitin, *Nations, States, and Violence* (Oxford: Oxford University Press, 2007), 31–49; or David. D. Laitin, 'Reply', *Nations and Nationalism* 2009 15(4): 566–573.

40. James Habyarimana et al., *Coethnicity: Diversity and the Dilemmas of Collective Action* (New York: Russell Sage Foundation, 2009), 103–104, 125.

41. Siniša Malešević, *The Sociology of Ethnicity* (London: Sage, 2004), 4

42. Richard Jenkins, *Rethinking Ethnicity: Arguments and Explorations*, 2nd edition (London: Sage, 2008), 14.

43. Steve Fenton, *Ethnicity* (Cambridge: Polity. 2003), 2, 113. Steve Fenton and the present author were close colleagues for twenty-three years. We agree upon many fundamentals but some of our philosophical differences have persisted from the beginning.

44. Sometimes members of indigenous groups present themselves as museum specimens and demand payment for being photographed. Sometimes they need protection from tourism companies. In 2012 the UN Committee on the Elimination of Race Discrimination inquired of the government of India about complaints that 'human safaris' for tourists were being driven through the Jawara Reserve in the Andaman Islands in possible breach of an order of the Supreme Court of India (UN document a/68/18 para 23).

45. John L. and Jean Comaroff, *Ethnicity, Inc.* (Chicago: University of Chicago Press, 2009), 60–85.

46. Andreas Wimmer, 'Does ethnicity matter? Everyday group formation in three Swiss immigrant neighbourhoods', *Ethnic and Racial Studies* 2004 27(1): 1–36.

7

Collective Action

In previous chapters it has been argued that much confusion surrounding the words 'race' and 'ethnicity' in sociology and political science can be cleared up by distinguishing practical from theoretical knowledge. Because it served political interests, race in the sense of the one-drop rule became one of the organizing principles in conceptions of the structure of US society. Attempts to give it a place in biological science had failed. First psychology and then economics found ways to build theoretical knowledge about social interaction in general, including black-white interaction, without being dependent upon any concept of race. How can sociology and political science follow their example?

Though psychology, economics, sociology and political science are distinctive disciplines that tackle particular kinds of intellectual problems, there are theories, such as those grouped as the theory of collective action, that can be employed in all these disciplines. Some versions can be used to account for differential behaviour on the basis of race, colour, descent and national or ethnic origin (the five grounds specified in the ICERD), plus those of religion and descent, because behaviour on all these seven grounds shares common features. These grounds are stated in emic terms. The social scientist has to seek explanations at a more fundamental level, employing etic concepts.

Theoretical knowledge grows by the development of intellectual traditions. In sociology one of the most influential traditions has been that deriving from the work of Max Weber, some of which shows him to have been an early pioneer of the theory of collective action. It can be educative to read the history of this, as of any other, theoretical perspective to see why some lines have prospered and why other possibilities have been overlooked or neglected.

The Rediscovery of Weber's 1911 Notes

After Max Weber's early death, a heap of manuscripts was found in his desk; many of them were incomplete, without definite titles or with no titles at all. Among them were two sets of pages apparently written about 1911 at a time when Weber was trying to identify 'universal types of groups' (like the household, the neighbourhood and the kin group) and was wondering whether characteristics of race, ethnic origin and nationality gave rise to the formation of such groups. Maybe he put these sheets of paper aside for possible use when he came back to these questions when writing a planned textbook. His widow, Marianne Weber, gave them a title, *Ethnische Gemeinsamkeitsbeziehungen*, and included them in the volume *Wirtschaft und Gesellschaft* as if they were a chapter her late husband had prepared for publication. Since the publication of the *Economy and Society* translations, in which the notes appear as part two, chapter V, on 'Ethnic Groups', passages from these notes have been reprinted in several volumes of readings about ethnic relations without any editorial explanation of their provisional character.[1]

Weber's over-riding interest was in the nature of *Gemeinschaft* and *Gesellschaft* (community and association) and in the factors, like the sharing of racial, ethnic and national origin, that led individuals to co-operate. In trying to define what had to be explained, Weber showed an acute awareness of the problematic nature of the ordinary language words available to identify the nature of these bonds. His comments on these apparently distinctive yet related social forms were so perceptive that they deserve careful consideration even after the passage of a hundred years. They bring together, for the first time, identification by race, by ethnic origin and by national origin, subsuming these emic constructs within an embryonic theory of collective action.

According to Weber, the source of the difference between community and association lay in the relationships of individuals[2]:

A social relationship will be called 'communal' (*Vergemeinschaftung*) if and in so far as the orientation of social action – whether in the individual case, on the average, or in the pure type – is based on a subjective feeling of the parties, whether affectual or traditional, that they belong together.

A social relationship will be called 'associative' (*Vergesellschaftung*) if and in so far as the orientation of social action within it rests on a rationally motivated adjustment of interests or a similarly motivated agreement, whether the basis of rational judgement be absolute values or reasons of expediency.

Communal relationships were exemplified by religious brotherhoods, erotic relationships, relations of personal loyalty, national communities, the *esprit de corps* of military units and by the family. Their members were bound together in what have been called 'multiplex' relations. The 'purest cases of associative relationships' were given as: free market exchange; a voluntary association oriented to 'specific ulterior interests'; and a voluntary association that seeks only to serve a cause.

Weber did not make this explicit, but he appears to have believed that while a subjective feeling creates a social relationship, that relationship also creates the feeling. The two are reciprocal, each determining the other. To write of an 'orientation' is to suggest that there is a subjective feeling or an intention that pairs with the obligation; they are like two sides of one coin. If that is the case, the two sentences could equally well have read:

> A subjective feeling will be called 'communal' when it is based on a set of social relationships such that the parties are involved with each other in multiple relationships.

> A subjective feeling will be called 'associative' when it is based on a social relationship with a very narrow range of obligations, such as those of a seller and a buyer.

If the subjective feeling and the objective relationship are reciprocal, Weber's statement can be simplified. When two persons interact, their conduct is governed by the norms of one or more social relationships. *Gesellschaftlich* relations are one-dimensional, governed by the norms of a single pair of roles. *Gemeinschaftlich* relations are multidimensional, governed by the norms of any pair of roles that the parties choose to play. Individuals do not normally choose to enter into communal relations; they are born into them, or find that they have entered them when they have entered into particular relationships, such as marriage, or, to quote one of Weber's examples, have joined a military unit.

Associative relations are formed for specific purposes; parties to them play specific roles. If they start to interact on the basis of other roles as well, the relations between the persons in question are no longer strictly associative, but are of a mixed character. Thus the contrast between community and association as polar opposites can be changed into a scale starting from one-dimensional relations up to a high point at which two parties identify with one another like identical twins. Multidimensionality is a variable.

Community living brings benefits and costs, both material and immaterial. Young adults may experience the pressure to conform as so great that they want to escape from it. They maintain their membership in their communities of origin so long as they believe the costs of exit to be greater than the benefits of remaining within the group. If they choose to live elsewhere, they may be able to retain a qualified membership.

Four Propositions

Later editors have placed first a page of Weber's that began by asking what might be meant by 'membership of a race'? It offered the answer that common descent only expresses itself in the form of a 'community' when the individuals concerned have a subjective feeling of their common identity that is supported by social relations between them. This emphasis on the subjective element was significant, for if Weber had thought that 'race' might be a universal type of group he would presumably have stressed objective characteristics and the word's horizontal dimension. Questioning whether there was anything distinctive about groups based on race, Weber answered that in the US southern states the whites' abhorrence of biracial marriage stemmed from their monopolization of social power and honour. This was a sociological explanation.

Then he generalized the explanation by noting, 'Any cultural trait can serve as a starting point for the familiar tendency to monopolistic closure.' He went on to assert that while almost any kind of similarity or opposition in habit and way of life could generate a belief that the sense of community sprang from some racial affinity, that belief might have no objective foundation. Its sources might lie elsewhere.

Weber observed that when a man 'is foreign in his external appearance', however he acted or whoever he might be, the primary and normal response was one of rejection. This was not due to any anthropological (or 'racial') difference; it could be a reaction to a cultural difference. His next pages took up the question of cultural difference as the basis for the formation of an ethnic group. They outlined four important and original propositions.[3] They may be expressed as follows:

1. We shall use the expression 'ethnic' groups to describe human groups (other than kinship groups) that cherish a belief in their common origins of such a kind that it provides a basis for the creation of a community;
2. The 'ethnic' group differs from the 'kinship group' in that it is constituted simply by the belief in a common identity, whereas a kinship group is a genuine 'community', characterised by genuinely communal activity;
3. By contrast, the sense of a common ethnic identity (as that expression is being used here) is not itself a community, but only something which makes it easier to form one;
4. Conversely, it is often the political community, even when formed in a highly artificial way, which gives rise to beliefs in ethnic identity.

The translation in *Economy and Society* used the potentially misleading expression 'ethnic membership'; this distracts attention from questions about the nature of the units of which people were members.[4] Weber focused on the sense of community with certain other persons who might be simply a set of individuals; whether they used this sentiment to change themselves from a category into a social group, and make 'membership' possible, was a further question. As the fourth proposition stated, it was not necessarily the sentiment that created the group. When a group had come into being, it could nurture a corresponding sentiment that contributed to its continuing existence.

Weber found a sense of shared ethnic origin to be associated with a miscellany of differences, linguistic and religious, with the experience of migration, with membership in a political unit like a tribe, with endogamous social circles concerned to defend their status, differences in clothing, style of housing, food, eating habits and the division of labour between the sexes. As if this was not confusing enough already, he added that 'what matters is precisely those things which may otherwise appear to be of only minor social importance'.

In the third chapter of *Economy and Society* there are translations of other pages, presented under the headings 'Tribe and Political Community: The Disutility of the Notion of "Ethnic Group"' and 'Nationality and Cultural Prestige'. Here Weber moved on to the third kind of potential group, the nation. He started from the proposition that 'the concept of "nationality" shares with that of the Volk (or "people") – in the "ethnic" sense – the vague connotation that whatever is felt to be distinctively common must derive from common descent'. But how did the nation differ from the ethnic group? Weber concluded that 'feelings of identity subsumed under the term "national" may derive from diverse sources'. 'Time and again we find that the concept "nation" directs us to political power'.

Where did Weber get his ideas about ethnic community? What stopped him distinguishing the 'ethnic' from the 'national'? That he felt unsure about these constructs can be seen from his liberal use of quotation marks. He seems to have been the first writer to wonder how an ethnic minority might differ from a national minority, or how 'ethnic origin' might differ from 'national origin'.

The answer to the first question may lie in Weber's four-month visit in 1904 to the United States. There he will have met many German-Americans, so he probably had them in mind when he wrote about how 'colonists' spiritual ties with their homeland survive'. He seems to have regarded German-Americans as an ethnic group rather than as a national group, because 'they have become so thoroughly adapted to their new environment that they themselves would find it intolerable to return to their old homes'.

Weber may have put his notes aside because he was dissatisfied with them. He had apparently been looking for a one-to-one relation between a sentiment and a social form, but found no separate sentiment that could promote a sense of shared nationality. Instead of identifying, and focusing upon, an observation that called for explanation, Weber listed some miscellaneous reports of observations and stated that a 'rigorous sociological analysis' of '"ethnically" determined action' would have to separate all the factors that could create ethnic attraction and repulsion; were this done, he noted, 'the collective term "ethnic" would be abandoned'.

The exercise led him to conclude that the concept of an *ethnische Gemeinschaft* 'which dissolves if we define our terms exactly, corresponds in this regard to one of the most vexing, since emotionally charged concepts: the nation, as soon as we attempt a sociological definition'.[5] There were two mistakes here. Firstly, the difference between the ethnic and the national had turned out to be one of circumstance, not of sentiment or *Gefühl*. Weber had failed to spot an intervening variable. Possibly unlike German-born people in Germany's African colonies, German-Americans constituted an ethnic rather than a national minority because their intention of remaining in the United States trumped their sense of being German. As already noted, in 1916 this issue became critical for them.

Shared ethnic origin can be a dimension of social life at different levels. There is the continental level, exemplified in the distinction between Europeans and Africans; there is the state, or national, level; and there is the substate level. Shared national origin has to be analysed both in relation to movements seeking the establishment of a state, and in relation to the maintenance of an existing state. At this level the other attributes of which a belief in shared national origin can serve as a sign are so important that they enforce a stronger conceptual distinction between state-oriented ethnic action and other ethnic action than is to be found in Weber's text.

Secondly, while Weber recognized that the sentiment, the *Gefühl,* had more influence in some situations than others, he did not build it into the four propositions noted above. Many sentiments are associated with relationships and the same person is involved in many relationships simultaneously. This has earlier been called multidimensionality. Two persons, A and B, may interact as man and woman, or as persons of the same gender. They can also interact as persons of the same, or different, social status, ethnic origin, citizenship, religious faith and so on. The number of possible dimensions to their relations is great indeed. A gender relationship is differentiated from a status relationship or an ethnic relationship by the parties' awareness of norms that define the nature of the relationship. A common ethnic origin may sponsor a norm in one relationship and not in another.

The communities that are considered relatively cohesive are the communities whose members relate to one another on a multiplicity of relationships. They are also the communities in which two or more social categories are very closely associated. The cases of Jews and Sikhs as formally defined by both ethnic origin and faith are well-known, but in many contact situations there is an expectation that ethnic origin and religion (or some other cultural characteristic) will go together. This association of categories is often called intersectionality. Its significance explains why the prominence given in the *Economy and Society* translation to the idea of 'membership' in an ethnic or national group is misleading. Real groups (as opposed to categories) are multidimensional.[5] There are both ethnic and national dimensions to a social relation if there are distinct ethnic and national norms of behaviour.

Seen in retrospect, one remarkable feature of Weber's 1911 thoughts about the nation is that neither then, nor in what appears in *Economy and Society* as chapter IX, 'Political Communities' (written at much the same time), does he consider the relation between the nation and the state. Nor does he comment on the relation between *Nationalgefühl* and territory; this is astonishing, considering how many 'national anthems' (which are sometimes state anthems) highlight the most distinctive features of those territories, and the identification evident in musical compositions celebrating 'my land' or 'our land'.

At the end of the chapter on 'Basic Sociological Terms', written shortly before his death, Weber has a sentence that is difficult to translate. In *Economy and Society* it appears as a definition of the state as 'a compulsory organization with a territorial basis'.[6] Weber had not revised his earlier statement that 'the concept [of the nation] belongs in the sphere of values', or investigated which values were relevant in this context.[7] Control of territory had not been an important issue in the unification of Germany in 1871; the circumstances of that unification may explain why Weber attributed less significance than other authors to a possible sense of shared territory, or to the association of state power with the control of territory; he gave more emphasis to shared descent and shared language as generators of national sentiment.

The link between the ethnic and the national in Weber's scheme was that they were both forms of political behaviour grounded in a sense of shared descent. The closeness of the link in ordinary language usage is exemplified in the ICERD's reference to 'national or ethnic origin'. It derives from the significance of the word 'ethnos' in classical Greek, from an era before the formation of nation states. The state is often regarded as a European concept dating from the Treaty of Westphalia in 1648. It counts the recognition of shared descent as the link between the citizen and the state. Many states in Asia do not use this as such a link. Nor is there a need for one in a technical language where the objective should be to identify a variable that can be measured. To link ethnic group with nation is to introduce the question of how the nation is related to the state. Is there an Arab nation distributed over several states? Are the Roma a nation without a state, or can any action in their name be accounted nationalist?

In Europe, a state is regarded as possessing a territory, and when Europeans established colonies in Africa they defined their new territory by drawing lines on a map that ignored the boundaries between ethnic groups. In near-desert conditions in East Africa, the borders drawn between Ethiopia, Kenya and Somalia disrupted the lives of pastoralists accustomed to moving with their camels or cows to whatever districts had benefited from the irregular rainfall of that region. The interaction between the administrative procedures of the state, and the utilization of state rules by the local people whenever it suited their interests, set in motion a process of ethnicization within Kenya's borders.[8] However, to qualify as a member of some ethnic groups, a person might have to qualify on more than one dimension of membership; in this region no one can now be counted as Somali unless he or she is a Muslim as well, resembling the Jewish and Sikh identifications of ethnic origin with religious profession.[9]

Closure

Before 1920, Weber had prepared for publication three chapters setting out what he called his *Kategorienlehre,* or doctrine of categories. This represented a new departure, inconsistent with the mode of explanation he had employed in his substantive writings on the world religions.[10] Just before his death, he wrote to his former pupil Robert Liefmann, an economist, 'If I now happen to be a sociologist according to my appointment papers, then I became one in order to put an end to the mischievous enterprise which still operates with collectivist concepts [*Kollektivbegriffe*].'[11] The three chapters on interpretive sociology were a first attempt to put an end to the mischievous enterprise. They started from 'the behaviour of one or more individual human beings' instead of from the sources of community. They outlined a bottom-up sociological theory as an alternative to the top-down theories that shaded into philosophies of history.

Weber had observed that a social relationship might be either open or closed to outsiders. An open relationship would be one in which someone was pursuing his or her personal interests in whatever directions they led. A closed relationship would be one seeking to develop collective action of an exclusive kind in pursuit of shared objectives. Thus trade union members could maximize their bargaining power by restraining 'competitive struggle within the group'. By voting for a closed shop, and imposing a rule upon themselves and their fellows, workers could maximize their average earnings – just as the whites in the southern states of the United States had engaged in collective action to the disadvantage of blacks. On the other hand, Weber wrote, 'If the participants expect that the admission of others will lead to an improvement of their situation, an improvement in degree, in kind, in the security or value of the satisfaction, their interest will be in keeping the relationship open.'[12] Their course would then be one of individual action.

It can be difficult to persuade industrial workers to support occupational closure. This was a starting point for one of the canonical works in the theory of collective action, Mancur Olson's 1965 book, *The Logic of Collective Action: Public Goods and the Theory of Groups.*[13] He observed that though collective bargaining on behalf of workers in a particular trade might secure them higher wages, an individual worker might calculate that he could benefit from such a raise without joining the union. He could be a 'free rider', benefiting from the collective action of others. To prevent this, a trade union might try to organize a 'closed shop', closing the trade to non-members. Some collective actions, like those of caste-based groups in India discussed in the previous chapter, make an imperative demand upon all their members.[14] There may be no free riders but plenty of captive travellers compelled to go along with the crowd.

Weber provided diverse examples of closure. Apart from those associated with economic relations, he noted that the choice of the language to be used would limit a conversation to those who could speak that language. Status groups often maintained linguistic peculiarities to keep themselves exclusive. If it was the language for a publication, though, closure would probably be expensive. There were degrees of closure; it could be higher for 'a theatrical audience the members of which have purchased tickets' than for 'a party rally to which the largest possible number has been urged to come'. 'Monopolistic closure' was the highest degree. In the competition for social status, some persons wished their groups to appear exclusive, and this required an emphasis on what made them distinctive. Characteristically, Weber added that the details about forms of closure and appropriation 'must be reserved for the later analysis'. He did not furnish comparable examples of the circumstances that occasion the opening of previously closed relationships. Maybe they too were reserved for later analysis.

That was never possible, and the absence of such an analysis has passed unnoticed. It was his writing on the sociology of religion and methodology that appealed most to other sociologists. The 1911 notes attracted less attention than his criticism of racial theories that claimed a foundation in biology. Then, in 1947, part of a chapter on which Weber had been working was published as 'Class, Status and Party'.[15] Particularly because of the publication of this translation, Weber came to be seen as the exponent of the analysis of racial and ethnic relations in terms of status rather than of class. The extract inspired John Rex to argue that the overarching sociological problem was the differential incorporation of racial and ethnic groups into the structures of the states in which they resided. In the process of incorporation, political and legal structures were as important as economic ones, and the groups interacted as classes.[16] When Siniša Malešević included in his text on *The Sociology of Ethnicity* a chapter on 'Neo-Weberian Theory: Ethnicity as a Status Privilege', he reviewed work inspired by the 'Class, Status and Party' text (now reprinted in *Economy and Society*, part one, chapter IV), not that which had been inspired by the chapter on 'Ethnic Groups'.[17]

In its application to the study of racial and ethnic relations, the theory of collective action must begin by recording the significance of values imparted during the process of socialization. According to this theory, actions can be explained as searches for maximum net advantage, comprehending psychic as well as material benefits, and recognizing that choices can be made only between the available alternatives. For the purposes of this book, the introductory argument can be expressed in three propositions:

1. During socialization, a human learns to identify with, and value association with, certain other persons.
2. In dealings with others, a person learns to maximize his or her net advantages, balancing both material and immaterial costs and benefits.
3. In such dealings, the person chooses between available alternatives.

For example, in the US Deep South, some alternatives that would elsewhere have been open to blacks were closed and any attempt to exercise them evoked punishment. Throughout the country, application of the one-drop rule restricted the freedom of individuals to identify themselves.

Seen from this standpoint, changes in the US census open up possibilities, in the practical realm, of further change resulting from individual choices. In the theoretical realm it invites more systematic study of the factors that cause individuals to present themselves in new ways, and thereby to increase or decrease the closure of relationships.

The Human Capital Variable

It was argued at the end of chapter 4 that interpersonal relations are multidimensional. Two individuals can interact on the basis of alternative social relationships, like those of gender, age, religion, socioeconomic class, language and so on. Particularly when there is a difference in power, one party may be willing to interact on the basis of one relationship only (e.g. a police officer questioning a motorist). Relations can be changed by a shift to a different relationship; this is easier when the individuals in question are members of local communities; these consist of persons who have varied individual characteristics but share a common life and have shared interests. Such a community may close itself off from other comparable communities.

Communities, in Weber's sense of groups bound by multiple ties, maintain a common life and are organized to defend it if necessary. What its members share is a form of social capital, one that facilitates transactions between its members. Definitions of social capital vary, but their core idea is the proposition that social networks have value, for both individuals and communities. So anything that facilitates individual or collective action (such as networks of relationships, reciprocity, trust and social norms) can be accounted social capital. It can be drawn upon for the pursuit of good ends or bad ends. Members of an ethnic or national majority hold some social capital in common. So do members of every social minority, whether religious, ethnic or territorial. The drawing of a color line or the observance of an ethnic boundary can prevent social transactions that would cross the line, while promoting relations within the social categories on either side of it. Ethnic diversity may therefore put brakes on economic performance that may not be counterbalanced by other benefits.

Research that makes use of these ideas about social capital may help the search for new etic constructs. National history can be read as a story of the accumulation, and sometimes the diminution, of social capital. Other experiences may outweigh any such influence, but in general, societies founded upon immigration, like the United States and Australia, can be expected to have less social capital than those that have been accustomed to emigration, like many West European countries. Both the United States and Australia developed with an immigrant conception of their national society. In very many other countries there is a population consisting of people who, if pressed, will say that they are the *Staatsvolk*, the original inhabitants and therefore the owners of the territory.[18] Most of the time they are not pressed. They are not obliged to think about who they are, and do not want to engage in what many regard as a pointless exercise. Majority-minority relations on the two sides of the Atlantic Ocean therefore differ in this connection.[19]

In most European countries, majority sentiment is inchoate and tacit. It is not easily investigated by survey methods because the shared sentiment is diffuse; in an opinion poll about people's concerns, it would yield place to more specific and immediate priorities. So its importance is easily underestimated.

In a landmark contribution to the study of social capital, Robert Putnam compared two theories. 'The first, usually labelled the "contact hypothesis", argues that diversity fosters interethnic tolerance and social solidarity.'[20] Yet Putnam thought it fair to observe that 'most (though not all) empirical studies have tended instead to support the so-called "conflict theory", which suggests that ... diversity fosters out-group distrust and in-group solidarity'. Whether contact promotes tolerance or conflict depends upon the kind of relationship within which the contact occurs, and the attitudes and expectations people hold before entering into contact. These theories cannot therefore be properly tested by opinion surveys carried out at a single moment in time. Survey methods can uncover associations but not their causes.

In the same lecture, Putnam also distinguished between bonding social capital ('ties to people who are like you in some way') and bridging capital ('ties to people who are unlike you in some way'). High bonding might be compatible with high bridging; he quoted a finding that US whites who have more white friends also have more non-white friends.

The concept of bonding capital has much in common with the concept of morale. It has long been recognized that a small military unit with high morale can often defeat a much larger one with low morale. Victory in a contest between sports teams may go to the one with greater team spirit. There can be an inspirational quality in interpersonal relations. Putnam argued that the central element in this quality, and in social capital, is that of generalized reciprocity. This, in turn, rests upon trust in others.[21] A major study in the Netherlands carried this argument further by examining the neighbourhood effects of ethnic, religious and economic diversity, plus Dutch-language proficiency, while allowing for the individual characteristics of respondents (such as educational levels). These were assessed against three scales measuring different forms of social trust: 'the first to the quality of contact, the second to trust in the neighbourhood and the third to trust between ethnic groups'.[22]

Putnam had concluded that in the United States ethnic heterogeneity was associated negatively with the quality of contact with neighbours. This finding was confirmed for the Netherlands, even after controlling for the effects of economic, religious and language differences. However, 'We do not find an association between ethnically diverse neighbourhoods and trust in the neighbourhood, neither for the immigrants nor for the natives.' Moreover, 'Ethnic diversity has a positive effect on the level of inter-ethnic trust of Dutch residents, but a negative effect on the quality of contact with neighbours for everybody'.[23]

Diversity in the neighbourhood did not necessarily have, for Dutch residents, the same sort of effect as variations in individual characteristics. Thus religious diversity decreased the quality of contact with neighbours, trust in the neighbourhood and interethnic trust. At the same time, a higher level of individual attendance at religious services increased the scores on all three indicators of trust. A further study in the Netherlands found that the theory of preferences and structural constraints can explain entry into intergroup contact among both immigrants and natives.[24] Economic diversity was associated with higher trust in the neighbourhood and higher interethnic trust among both immigrant and native residents. The authors suggested that economic differences can be 'synergetic'. By this they apparently mean that 'people with a different ethnic background are less likely to compete with one another'. They may even be complementary: 'a consultant needs a bakery, and a renter profits from the owner renovating his house and making the street more attractive to live in'. [25]

A recent study of social cohesion in local communities in Britain found no evidence that racial diversity had an eroding effect upon social interaction once allowance had been made for the association between racial diversity and economic deprivation. At the same time it reported a 'puzzling' finding that racial diversity had a direct negative effect on the perceptions of, and trust in, fellow neighbours.[26] Further research results may modify conclusions of this kind. Much may turn on whether perceptions of neighbours are derived from personal experience rather than from the mass media.

An analysis of relative ethnic, linguistic and religious heterogeneity in states of the OECD (Organisation for Economic Co-operation and Development) found ethnic fractionalization to be a significant predictor of economic performance.[27] It did not identify the causes of the observed association. Those who pioneered this mode of analysis traced the negative effects of ethnic fractionalization to ethnic differences in preferences for alternative forms of public expenditure.[28]

The findings of empirical research are in general compatible with the argument that multidimensional social relations embody more social capital than unidimensional relations because they facilitate reciprocity. They suggest that the sentiments that can make a *Staatsvolk* appear distinctive stem from the same source. Moreover, they point to possible ways in which such a mode of explanation may be developed.

Probably the biggest weakness of some of the available studies that were designed to test 'contact theory' is that the techniques currently available to measure the effects of contact are very weak. There are great advantages in examining instead actual changes in behaviour, such as the decisions made by individuals who could identify with more than one line of ancestry. A technique for measuring preferences for association with co-ethnics could be adapted to measure the effects of contact.

The Colour Variable

Another variable influential at both the interpersonal and the global levels is the significance accorded to shades of skin colour. In the United States, discrimination on grounds of colour is treated as a form of racial discrimination; nevertheless both backs and whites sometimes discriminate on grounds of colour. Analysis of data obtained in the New Immigrant Survey 2003 (of 8,573 respondents) found that, after controlling for the effects of education, English language proficiency, occupation in source country, family background, ethnicity, race and country of birth, immigrants with the lightest skin colour (measured on a eleven-point scale) earned on average 17 per cent more than immigrants with the darkest skin colour. An additional unit of skin colour darkness on the scale lowered wages by 1.7

per cent (while an additional inch of height above the US gender-specific average brought a wage advantage of 2 per cent).[29] Many of the employers who were displaying a preference for lighter-skinned and taller employees will have been white. There were also many allegations that African American supervisors and fellow workers discriminated on the basis of skin colour, both of the lighter-skinned discriminating against the darker-skinned and vice-versa.[30] The Equal Employment Opportunity Commission was taking many such cases to court.

A very substantial body of evidence has been accumulated attesting to the existence of a preference for a light skin colour preference within the African American population. In what are perceived as black-white encounters, black solidarity may be strong. When this opposition is absent, other distinctions can come to the fore. Colour preference is often referred to as 'colorism'. Some African Americans underestimate its significance because they do not wish to air what they regard as dirty laundry in public, as if the issue were African American property.[31] Insofar as that is the case, it is a consequence of the so-called one-drop rule. Despite this sensitivity, recent research has gone beyond the earlier studies reporting that infants prefer light-coloured dolls to dark-coloured ones, and that light-coloured females have an advantage in the rating-dating complex. In particular, a national survey of Black Americans has found that among African American women who are judged as having 'low and average levels of attractiveness', self-esteem is associated with lighter skin colour. Self-esteem was not found to be associated with lightness of complexion among women judged 'highly attractive' or of higher socio-economic status. The influence of skin tone effect among women operated through its consequences for income and education. Differences in skin tone effect were associated with the feeling of self-efficacy among men at twice the rate among women.[32]

African Americans with fairer complexions report higher earnings than darker-complexioned persons. The same survey found that for every dollar earned by a light-skinned African American, a darker-skinned person earned 72 cents. A further finding was that African Americans with a light skin tone were more likely to be married than those with a dark complexion, by a difference of 42 to 27 per cent. The spouses of light-skinned respondents had average earnings of $21,540; of respondents with medium complexions, $20,332; and of those with dark complexions, $17,510. The differences in the social experience of African Americans can be traced to the ways in which other Americans treat them.[33]

These findings are consistent with the hypothesis that the colour preferences of white Americans have been absorbed into a colour scale governing employment. Other findings support the hypothesis that those disadvantaged by such a scale draw upon their shared experience to construct a scale of their own when they mobilize for political action at the national level or develop ideas of a racial or ethnic identity in interpersonal relations. For example, some people may be considered 'not black enough' to represent African Americans. In these circumstances there may be a colour scale in which a dark black complexion is at the top of the scale and a white one is at the bottom. There are also indications that in very 'mixed' societies some people identify with a midpoint as best representative of the whole population. Advertising agencies may prefer to engage models with intermediate complexions for similar reasons, and the practice of tanning shows that in some circumstances a fair complexion is preferred to a pale one.[34]

The idea of a colour scale has the virtue of generality. It can be manifested in all regions of the world. Sometimes, the whiter a person's skin colour, the higher he or she is ranked. In other countries, or in other circumstances, the blackest persons are ranked highest, while elsewhere an intermediate complexion may be regarded the most favourably. The social significance attributed to a position on such a scale varies with the social relationship; in some relationships it may be zero or even carry a minus value. A colour scale is usually a component of a larger scale of socio-economic status. Other physical characteristics, such as hair form, can be involved.

Describing the system of continuous differentiation in Jamaica around 1950, Stuart Hall testified: 'Anybody in my family could compute and calculate anybody's social status by grading the particular quality of their hair versus the particular quality of the family they came from and which street they lived in, including physiognomy, shading, etc. You could trade off one characteristic against another.'[35] In Jamaica at this time the banks and other commercial establishments recruited staff of fair complexion for positions involving contact with members of the public. In this respect, the practice resembled the colour-based social differentiation practiced within the US black population, particularly before the Civil Rights era. The research worker who seeks to account for such forms of differentiation finds other concepts to be more useful than racism.

In Britain in the 1950s, there was a general tendency among whites to see the population as divided into 'white or coloured'. Following the trend in the United States, there was, from the 1960s, increased self-identification as 'black', yet two outstanding British athletes whom others would have considered black refused to be included in a book about black sportsmen, one on the grounds that he had an English mother and thought this would be an insult to her, the other, who had been fostered in a rural area by another white parent, insisted, 'I may be black but this is not the most important thing about me.'[36]

The possibility of 'identity change' depends upon the options available. If, in the United Kingdom, a person of both black and white parentage refuses to align himself or herself according to the one-drop rule, the social costs of such a decision are likely to be much lower than they might be in the United States. In the United Kingdom, any colour line has been incorporated to a greater extent into the assessment of socio-economic status; non-white minorities have, relatively speaking, been numerically small, and there have been no urban ghettos. Attitudes have long been more fluid than in the United States. This fluidity was not always seen as beneficial when the author was conducting research in London in 1950–52. Several times he heard black men complain that 'in America, you know where you stand; here you never know what to expect'.

Ethnic Preferences

Preferences for association with co-ethnics can be expected among members of any ethnic group.[37] These preferences will not necessarily be of positive value. In some circumstances people wish to avoid co-ethnics. Their preferences will then be of negative value. Because persons on both sides of a colour-based distinction tend to identify collectively, the possibility of their having co-ethnic neighbours may influence their search for housing and the possibility of their children having co-ethnic classmates may affect their choice of schools. These are only preferences, so there will be a trade-off against other values.

A technique for measuring such preferences was developed for use in surveys in which samples of urban Malaysians have been interviewed. Subjects were asked to predict how they thought others would decide in situations designed to measure preference for association with co-ethnics relative to the alternatives of personal gain and desire to meet what was felt as a personal obligation. In one situation they were told that Husin Ali, a representative Malay-Malaysian, bought his groceries from Ah Kow's grocery shop, noted for its cheapness and close to his house. He had been told that someone called Ahmad was about to open a second grocery in the neighbourhood. Respondents were asked whether they thought that Husin Ali would transfer his custom to the new shop. Nothing in the interview said that Husin Ali was of Malay origin, or Ah Kow of Chinese origin. Those interviewed will have made this inference. In research elsewhere, the names or photographs of representative persons can be varied to discover more about the processes of social cognition.[38]

There was a common belief that Chinese-origin shopkeepers sold groceries more cheaply. Would Husin Ali prefer to help his co-ethnic (Ahmad), or would he buy where prices were lower (Ah Kow)? Were he to patronize Ahmad, this would be taken as an expression of social alignment based upon a preference for association with a co-ethnic. The strength of such a preference could be measured, for example, by finding whether Husin Ali was predicted to continue shopping with Ahmad, if, other things being equal, his prices were 2, 4, 6 or 8 per cent higher. In a shopping situation, some individuals will have a preference of zero for association with a co-ethnic; others may have a higher preference, depending perhaps upon their personalities, their financial circumstances or the social pressures they experience.

A prediction that Husin Ali would prefer to shop with his co-ethnic could be seen as an estimation of his individual likes and dislikes, or as reflecting his solidarity with the co-ethnics who have made him the person he is. This latter aspect was measured in the research by asking respondents how they thought Husin Ali's mother would wish him to act in the situations studied. The questions were varied to measure the preference for association with a co-ethnic by comparison with an expected financial gain, a gain in social status and the sense of obligation to a fellow employee. They were repeated in a study of the predicted ethnic preferences of a Chinese-Malaysian.

Just as many individuals will have a preference, in given situations, for association with a co-ethnic, so they may have preferences for association with someone of the same national origin, the same religion, the same gender, the same social class or a speaker of the same language. Questions could be devised that would enable an investigator to measure the strength of one such association relative to others. The components of forms of behaviour that have been aggregated as 'racial' can be separated. Methods of this kind provide better predictions of likely behaviour than the sorts of question posed in questionnaire research.

Where do ethnic preferences come from? Every child is inducted into a pre-existing network of kin, neighbours and acquaintances from whom he or she can expect support. So preferences for association with certain kinds of other people exist from an early age. They persist only if they are reinforced by everyday experiences of reciprocity. It is on this basis that sets or groups of persons sharing similar values take shape. Andreas Wimmer has investigated the process by reanalysing information in the European Social Survey, a data set with more than 100,000 individuals and 380 ethnic groups in 24 countries. He found that only between 2 and 3 per cent of the variation in the measured values was located at the level of the ethnic group; between 7 and 16 per cent occurred at the level of the country, and between 80 and 90 per cent at the level of the individual. Individuals who reported Islam as their religion did not diverge from the basic values of their countries any more than did Catholics.

The analysis showed that immigrants carried with them the value orientations into which they had been socialized, but that political exclusion had no effect on the value orientation of first-generation settlers. In the second generation, matters were very different. In the groups experiencing political exclusion, second-generation respondents deviated from the measured values three times more than their peers in groups that were not excluded. This supported the thesis that social closure increases the sharing of values in an excluded group.

Earlier in this book, it was held that many social relations are multidimensional, in that someone who has been playing one role can switch to another role. Communities are characterized by the diversity of the bases on which members can interact with one another. Wimmer takes this argument further by identifying four processes (he calls them mechanisms) by which different relationships can be tied with one another: availability, propinquity, homophily (or membership sharing) and balancing processes. Their influence is measured by use of a data set recording the social ties revealed by 1,640 students at a private college in the United States, 736 of whom posted photographs of their friends on Facebook.

This enabled Wimmer and his team to discover the existence of seventeen different communities, some ethnic, some based on the subjects studied and some tying together fans of particular bands or styles of music. The team concluded that 'racial homophily does not represent the prime principle of tie formation ... despite the emphasis on "race" that we find in many lay and sociological accounts of American society'.[39] The research opened up new techniques for comparing the strength of preferences for association with co-ethnics relative to other sentiments and ties governing the formation of social bonds.

Opening Relationships

Max Weber maintained, 'If the participants expect that the admission of others will lead to an improvement of their situation ... their interest will be in keeping the relationship open', whereas if 'their expectations are of improving their position by monopolistic tactics, their interest is in a closed relationship'. As has already been noted, he believed that the colour line in the US South represented a white 'monopolization of social power and honour'.[40] That action evoked, in the Civil Rights movement, a corresponding movement of closure on the part of blacks.

The statement of F. James Davis in 1991, quoted in chapter 2, that 'the one-drop rule is now as fully accepted in the black community as a whole as it is in the white community' may, in part, have reflected a feeling among black Americans that 'racial' solidarity is a form of social capital. Awareness of shared experience based on racial classification can be a better basis for a mobilization movement than an awareness of distinctions of colour, since those distinctions highlight individual differences. Whatever the belief, it does not long remain in force unless it is confirmed by daily experience, and is not challenged by new alternatives appealing to the participants' personal interests.

Any opening of the black-white relationship in the United States can be regarded as a reflection of changing interests only if the word 'interest' is seen as reflecting more than economic interests. It must comprehend individuals' conceptions of their identities as citizens of a state and as human beings. Eugene Robinson's book *Disintegration* suggests that forms of identification are becoming more complicated.

The change in the US census by which individuals can now identify themselves as being of more than one race, and the movement to popularize 'multiracial' (or something similar) as an identification, makes available a new alternative. Research into people's decisions (whites as well as blacks) to identify, or not to identify, as being of more than one race, will throw light onto the opening of a previously closed relationship. The degree of openness-closure is another variable that bears upon ethnic relations.

The study of ethnic preferences offers a method for measuring the relative strength of both material and non-material interests. The studies in Malaysia asked whether a subject would define certain situations as requiring conformity to a norm of alignment with a co-ethnic, or whether they would set this aside in favour of their personal advantage, either in terms of money or identification with someone of higher social status, or whether they would observe a norm of social obligation to a neighbour or workmate. The underlying hypothesis was that subjects can draw satisfaction both from complying with norms and from personal advantage. They may trade off the satisfactions of personal gain against those of norm observance. It is not difficult to measure the relative strength of expected satisfactions. Modern market economies are based upon financial incentives; they weaken traditional forms of social categories and they loosen the association of categories. Much new technology works in ways independent of social distinctions and therefore weakens them. Research into the strength of civic norms relative to other norms and incentives should be of wider interest because the opening of social relationships should lead to an increase in social capital.

Use of this kind of technique may open up possibilities for comparing the significance attributed, in specific settings, to various kinds of physical difference, like skin colour, hair, height and weight, and to compare them with the significance attributed to social class, presentation of self and so on.

This book contends that sociology is a distinctive field insofar as there is a body of specifically sociological knowledge. It has invoked Durkheim's analysis of variations in suicide rates in support of the claim that there is distinctively sociological knowledge (though much of it is shared with other social sciences). Durkheim demonstrated that some of these variations were determined by factors of which the parties were not conscious. Some of the best research into racial and ethnic relations – like the US studies of caste and class in the Deep South in the 1930s – has similarly shown how the participants' lives could be structured by social institutions when those concerned often had only limited understanding of the system within which they lived. These studies added to sociological knowledge about how two-category social systems can work even if the circumstances in the Deep South have since changed.

The further growth of sociological knowledge in this field would surely benefit from locating the intellectual problems, the explananda, within a larger historical and conceptual framework. The field began as an attempt to account for the social significance attributed to phenotypical differences among humans. Those were differences of physique, particularly of complexion and hair. Significance is a relative matter, so the attention paid to physical characteristics had to be considered alongside differences of religion, language, gender and national or ethnic origin. Further progress will depend upon the construction of a framework for explaining the significance attributed, in different sections of a population, to cultural as well as physical differences.

The discovery of etic constructs to supersede the emic constructs of race and ethnicity will not come from research designed as a search for successor concepts, but will be a by-product of research designed to meet other objectives, such as research into the trade-off between ethnic preferences and other preferences, or into the sources of social capital. Research that is not dependent on ordinary language concepts of race and ethnicity will bring the study of racial and ethnic relations into closer relation with sociological research in general.

Notes

1. Max Weber, *Wirtschaft und Gesellschaft. Grundriss der Verstehenden Soziologie*, 1st edition, (1921); 5th edition, edited by Johannes Winkelmann (Tübingen: Mohr Siebeck); *Economy and Society: An Outline of Interpretive Sociology*, edited by Guenther Roth and Claus Wittich, translations by various authors (New York: Bedminster, 1968); *Wirtschaft und Gesellschaft: die Wirtschaft und die gesellschaftlichen Ordnungen und Mächte; Nachlass. Teilbd. 1. Gemeinschaften*, edited by Wolfgang J. Mommsen; *Gesamtausgabe. Bd.22. Abteilung 1. Schriften und Reden* (Tübingen: Mohr, 2001).
2. Weber, *Economy and Society*, 40–41.
3. Quoted here from W. G. Runciman, *Selections in Translation*, edited by Max Weber (Cambridge: Cambridge University Press, 1978), 364, because its translation of them is better than that in *Economy and Society*, 389. Some passages in this section also appear in Michael Banton, 'Updating Max Weber on the Racial, the Ethnic and the National', *Journal of Classical Sociology* 2014 14(3): 325–340.

4. Weber, *Economy and Society*, 395.
5. The word 'group' is an emic construct used in different senses. A statistician may group certain observations using the verbal form, and then refer to the resulting set as a group, using the noun. A psychologist may assemble a set of individuals as an experimental group, although its members have no continuing relations with each other. A social group is said to exist when a set of individuals are conscious of belonging to a continuing unit. Many references to 'ethnic groups' relate to ethnic categories.
6. Weber, *Economy and Society*, 56. The original reads: 'Verbandsgenossen, sondern im weiten Umfang für alles auf dem beherrschten Gebiet stattfindende Handeln (also: gebietsanstaltsmäßig)'. As translator, Talcott Parsons took away the parentheses in an attempt to extract its meaning (56).
7. Ibid., 922. Weber made little use of any concept of society; he might have associated its use with 'the mischievous enterprise which still operates with collectivist concepts'. Weber's basic concepts were those of *gemeinschaft* and *gesellschaft* which are usually represented in English as community and association; 'society' (as in the title *Economy and Society*) is not a true equivalent of *gesellschaft*, but the closest approximation.
8. Günther Schlee, 'Territorializing ethnicity: The imposition of a model of statehood on pastoralists in northern Kenya and southern Ethiopia', *Ethnic and Racial Studies* 2013 36(5): 857–874; also Günther Schlee and Abdullahi A. Shongolo, *Pastoralism and Politics in Northern Kenya & Southern Ethiopia* (Woodbridge: James Currie, 2012).
9. Günther Schlee, *Islam & Ethnicity in Northern Kenya & Southern Ethiopia* (Woodbridge: James Currie, 2012), 7.
10. Mary Fulbrook, 'Max Weber's "Interpretive Sociology": A comparison of conception and practice', *British Journal of Sociology* 1978 29(1): 71–82.
11. H. H . Bruun, *Science, Values and Politics in Max Weber's Methodology* (Copenhagen: Munksgaard, 1972), p. 38).
12. Weber, *Economy and Society*, 43–44.
13. Mancur Olson, *The Logic of Collective Action: Public Goods and the Theory of Groups* (Cambridge MA: Harvard University Press, 1965).
14. Donald L. Horowitz, *The Deadly Ethnic Riot* (Berkeley: University of California Press, 2001).
15. Max Weber, *From Max Weber: Essays in Sociology*, edited by H. H. Gerth and C. Wright Mills (London: Kegan Paul, 1947), 180–195.
16. John Rex, 'The role of class analysis in the study of race relations – a Weberian perspective', in Rex and David Mason (eds.), *Theories of Race and Ethnic Relations* (Cambridge: Cambridge University Press, 1986), xii, 64–83.
17. Siniša Malešević, *The Sociology of Ethnicity*.
18. Georg Jellinek, *Allgemeine Staatslehre* (Berlin: Springer, 3rd ed. 1921, 1st ed. 1900).
19. In a comment on Taylor's *Multiculturalism and 'The Politics of Religion'*, 99–101, Michael Walzer draws a distinction between two kinds of liberalism. The first kind is 'committed in the strongest possible way to individual rights and a rigorously neutral state. The second kind is committed to the survival and flourishing of a particular nation, culture or religion ... so long

as the basic rights of citizens who have different commitments or no such commitments at all are protected.' Nation-states are of the latter kind: 'All nation-states act to reproduce men and women of a certain sort: Norwegian, French, Dutch, or whatever', so there is bound to be 'conflict with the efforts of minorities to sustain themselves over time'. The United States, like other 'immigrant societies', is of the former kind, in which 'there is no privileged majority and there are no exceptional minorities'. To this may be added the observation that in all countries the national bond is a source of social capital; that the bond is political in character, but that where, as in Norway, France and the Netherlands, it has deep cultural roots, it is likely to be stronger.

20. Robert Putnam, 'E Pluribus Unum: Diversity and Community in the Twenty-first Century', *Scandinavian Political Studies* 2007 30: 137–174.

21. Following James S. Coleman, *Foundations of Social Theory* (Cambridge, MA: Harvard University Press, 1990), 318–321.

22. Bram Lancee and Jaap Dronkers, 'Ethnic, Religious and Economic Diversity in Dutch Neighbourhoods: Explaining Quality of Contact with Neighbours, Trust in the Neighbourhood and Inter-Ethnic Trust', *Journal of Ethnic and Migration Studies* 2011 37(4): 597–618, at 603.

23. Ibid., 615.

24. Borja Martinović, 'The Inter-Ethnic Contacts of Immigrants and Natives in the Netherlands: A Two-Sided Perspective', *Journal of Ethnic and Migration Studies* 2013 39(1): 69–85.

25. Lancee and Dronkers, 'Ethnic, Religious and Economic Diversity', 601.

26. Natalia Letki, 'Does Diversity Erode Social Cohesion? Social Capital and Race in British Neighbourhoods', *Political Studies* 2008 56(1): 99–126.

27. Natalka Patsiurko, John L. Campbell and John A. Hall, 'Measuring cultural diversity: Ethnic, linguistic and religious fractionalization in the OECD', *Ethnic and Racial Studies* 2012 35(2): 195–217.

28. Rachel M. Gisselquist, 'Ethnic Divisions and Public Goods Provision, Revisited', *Ethnic and Racial Studies* 2014 37(9): 1605–1627.

29. Joni Hersch, 'Profiling the New Immigrant Worker: The Effects of Skin Color and Height', *Journal of Labor Economics* 2008 26(2): 345–386.

30. Kathy Russell, Midge Wilson and Ronald Hall, *The Color Complex: The Politics of Skin Color Among African Americans* (New York: Harcourt Brace Jovanovich, 1992), 124–134.

31. Ibid., 163.

32. Maxine S. Thompson and Verna M. Keith, 'Copper Brown and Blue Black: Colorism and Self-Evaluation', in Cedric Herring, Verna Keith and Hayward Derrick Horton (eds.), *Skin/Deep: How Race and Complexion Matter in the "Color-Blind" Era* (Chicago: University of Illinois Press, 2004), 45–64, 53–59.

33. Korie Edwards, Katrina M. Carter-Tellison and Cedric Herring, 'For Richer, For Poorer, Whether Dark or Light: Skin Tone, Marital Status, and Spouse's Earnings', in ibid., 65–81.

34. For a very interesting US study that failed to find any strong preferences as to skin colour among persons purchasing sperm, see Carol S. Walther, 'Skin

tone, biracial stratification and tri-racial stratification among sperm donors', *Ethnic and Racial Studies* 2014 37(3): 517–536.

35. Stuart Hall, 'Old and New Identities, Old and New Ethnicities', in Les Back and John Solomos (eds.), *Theories of Race and Racism: A Reader* (London: Routledge, 2000), 144–153, at 149.

36. Michael Banton, *Promoting Racial Harmony* (Cambridge: Cambridge University Press, 1983), 91.

37. In writing about black-white relations in the United States, the word 'preference' is used to denote special privileges for persons in particular categories. Here it is used in the sense that someone may be said to prefer to drink coffee without sugar.

38. Michael Banton, 'Ethnic Conflict', *Sociology* 2000 34(3): 481–498, reporting some of the findings in Mohd-Noor Mansor, 'The Determinants of Malay Ethnic Alignment', unpublished PhD dissertation, University of Bristol, 1992. There are advantages in asking subjects how a member of their peer group would behave in a typical situation rather than asking them how they themselves would behave in a situation that, for them, may appear too improbable. A key requirement is that it should not be the experimenter who introduces any social categorization – that is for the subject. A subject can be given a photograph, or told the name of another person, and asked how he or she would behave towards that person in a given situation. The experimenter can than infer whether the appearance, the name or anything else evokes categorization and differential behaviour.

39. Andreas Wimmer, *Ethnic Boundary Making: Institutions, Power, Networks* (Oxford: Oxford University Press, 2013), 141, 173, 175, 195, 199.

40. Weber, *Economy and Society*, 43, 386.

The Paradox Resolved

This book opened with references to the statement on race from the American Sociological Association in 2002. That statement can be read as a summary account of what US sociologists knew about race at that time.

The director of the Association stated that race was a changing social construct that 'shapes social ranking, access to resources, and life experiences'. It was a construct *used* in ways that had these effects.[1] The full statement declared that race was

A sorting mechanism for mating, marriage and adoption;

A stratifying practice for providing or denying access to resources;

An organizing device for mobilization to maintain or challenge systems of racial stratification;

A basis for scientifically investigating proximate causes.

Sociological research had shown that race was related to workplace inequalities, to residential segregation and to persistent differences in life expectancy and the incidence of particular sources of ill health.

To this was added a warning that refusal to employ racial categories in the collection of data would not eliminate their use by members of the public. 'In France, information about race is seldom collected officially, but evidence of systematic racial discrimination remains', and there was reference to experience in other countries. This observation introduced additional issues. The parallels with the problems of data collection may be close, but the variables to be measured in different countries are not at all the same. The ASA's 2002 conception of race in the United States cannot be generalized to other countries. Nevertheless, the similarities and dissimilarities should be of great interest to the sociologist.

This book has contended that what 'we' (all of us in the Western world) now know about race includes much more than knowledge at a particular point in time (like, say, the percentages of blacks and whites holding electoral office). It includes knowledge about historical or out-of-date uses of the word 'race', and knowledge of why these have been abandoned in favour of newer uses. This is sociological knowledge as opposed to knowledge organized to serve the purposes of social policy. Any such account leaves us with a challenge: given that we know a lot about the subject, should we regard it as knowledge about race, or as knowledge about some thing or things that we have not yet properly defined? Does not the study of human variation, physical and cultural, constitute a better starting point?

What we now know about ethnicity raises similar issues. The concept of an ethnic group was introduced for practical purposes. In public life it helped identify distinctive sections of the population (like hyphenated Americans). Within social science it helped identify culturally distinctive social categories (like, say, Hausa, Ibo and Yoruba in Nigeria). The difficulties that arose in equating race in the United States with race in France, and with generalizing about racism, were repeated when sociologists asked if there might be something to be called ethnicity that helped explain what distinguished ethnic groups from other kinds of group. Does our current knowledge about what distinguishes these groups constitute knowledge about ethnicity, or knowledge about something that we have not yet been able to define adequately?

These problems are the more testing because questions of race and ethnicity have parallels in the study of nationalism and other sources of social division. One possibility canvassed in chapter 4, and subsequently, is that it would be best to follow Max Weber's lead and concentrate on what it is that stimulates individuals to identify with others and to engage in collective action when this suits their purposes. Such a strategy would reinforce the emic/etic distinction, assigning race and ethnicity to the realm of practice while impelling social scientists to seek better concepts for their technical vocabulary.

A focus upon social science knowledge will have a distinctive quality in underlining the provisional nature of what passes as knowledge at any particular time. Study of how our knowledge has grown should teach lessons that will help us acquire further knowledge.

For knowledge to grow, we need words. A person who advances a new argument has to employ the vocabulary that is familiar to those he or she wishes to address. This often means taking a word in ordinary language and using it in a new sense, as, for example, the word 'nation' has been used for new purposes. The word's meanings multiply, as, in this example, they give rise to expressions like 'nationalism' (which is not easily defined). Those who seek to systematize the new knowledge then propose technical definitions that serve a special function.

A review of the scientific sources of the paradox (in chapter 1) concluded that towards the end of the eighteenth century a new kind of knowledge about race began to take shape. It was a form of theoretical knowledge, different in character from the practical use of the word to identify either a line of ancestry or, more simply, a set of persons. Some writers tried to persuade their readers that race was a valuable addition to the scientific vocabulary. Because science seeks a special kind of knowledge, based on causal explanation, they had to formulate a nominalist rather than a realist definition of race. It had to improve on the Linnaean taxonomy that centred on the concept of species, and to contribute to the discovery of new knowledge about the origin of species. This initiative demonstrably failed. Furthermore, the very concept of species became questionable. To explain the operation of natural selection, Darwin's hypothesis of inheritance as a process of the blending of ancestral qualities was superseded by Mendel's discovery of the inheritance of particulate qualities. Superior explanations banished their predecessors and laid the foundations upon which new theoretical knowledge was systematized.

Scientists are sometimes no better than non-scientists at abandoning ideas that have been outdated. Darwin and Mendel had destroyed the prevailing doctrine that knowledge grew by induction. According to one philosophy, the research worker's task was to assemble observations or specimens and classify them. From this process new knowledge in the form of explanations or theories was expected to emerge in some unspecified manner.[2] Some twentieth-century sociologists clung to this doctrine. Thus W. Lloyd Warner introduced his study of Yankee City with the declaration:

> In general, the three characteristic activities of modern science are the observation of 'relevant' phenomena, the arrangement of the facts collected by such observation into classes and orders, and the explanation of the ordering and classification of the collected data by means of so-called laws and principles. These several observations, ideally speaking, tend to take place in the described sequence. For example, our scientific knowledge of the heavenly bodies began with the observation of the different positions of the planets and their relative position to each other. Later classification

showed that the planets moved around the sun, and, still later, the 'law of gravitation' grouped the observed phenomena and their classification into one formula.[3]

This interpretation of progress in cosmology found no place for the imagination of geniuses like Copernicus and Galileo.

Nor did it reflect the working methods of Charles Darwin. In 1834, at the age of twenty-three and in the course of his voyage on the Beagle, he noticed seashells on a plain in Patagonia 330 feet above sea level. The geology books he had read provided no good explanation for their presence. Darwin hypothesized that they were there because the land level had been elevated by geological action. This inference was a key step in the development of his thinking about processes of evolution. After his return to Britain he tested his hypotheses in a series of small experiments, many of them in his garden in the village of Downe. There, in a letter to a friend, he remarked: 'How odd it is that anyone should not see that all observation must be for or against some view if it to be of service.'

This method of research is at the heart of the philosophy of critical rationalism pioneered by the Austrian-born philosopher of science, Karl Popper. He emphasized the importance of distinguishing between what was to be explained, the explanandum, and that which did the explaining, the explanans. He has stressed the importance of conjecture and refutation in the discovery of new knowledge. In sociology there are advantages in thinking more simply of the logic of question and answer because this draws attention to the difficulty of finding a good research question in sociology, something equivalent to Darwin's puzzlement over the sea shells, as opposed to a question concerning social policy.[4]

While the claims for race as a possible concept in science were being debated, the word was put to new uses in the realm of practical knowledge where it had a history of use in popular literature, and in the everyday need of a means for classifying the different sections of North America's growing population. In the United States, as chapter 2 insisted, racial categorization was the product not of slavery but of its abolition. It took the place of categorization as free or slave. By the late nineteenth century, the word 'race' had secured an established place in ordinary language, becoming the default position. The one-drop rule came to be accepted by blacks as well as whites. Race in this new sense gained so strong a hold on the thinking of academics as well as members of the public that too little thought was given to its use as an intellectual tool. It was utilized in new areas while retreating from others, for with technological innovations and a greater assimilation of local community life into national life, more situations have been socially defined in ways to which the black-white distinction is irrelevant.

The political use of racial categorization in Nazi Germany was accounted one of the causes of World War II. Chapter 3 summarized the steps by which, after that war, action against racial discrimination became part of international human rights law, most notably in the International Convention on the Elimination of All Forms of Racial Discrimination. The treaty obligations assumed by states parties, and the manner in which fulfilment of their obligations is monitored, are not yet properly appreciated by social scientists. The ICERD has become 'a living instrument' addressing new political issues. The Convention and these procedures drew upon, and added to, practical knowledge.

The growth of social science knowledge about race and ethnicity depends upon institutional support, notably in academic institutions. Chapter 4 summarized how the lead came from the University of Chicago's department of sociology under Robert E. Park. He had two intellectual predecessors. One was Max Weber, who had discussed the way in which a sense of shared racial, ethnic or national origin could promote community identification and action. The other was W. E. B. Du Bois, who had written what is considered the first sociological monograph and had described the international colour line. Neither of them had the institutional support to develop a research programme like Park's. The impetus to the growth of knowledge was all US-based.

Park did not start from the US ordinary language conception of 'race relations'. He sought a more general conceptual framework, but the ordinary language conception was too strong for him and the sociologists who learned from him. By the late 1930s, for lack of a better, 'race relations' had become their central organizing idea. Thereafter, the history of this field of study can be read as a sequence of efforts to find a better framework. None of the attempts so far has succeeded. The task is enormously difficult.

In his studies of the organization of social life in the Deep South, Warner minimized reference to race by relying on conceptions first of caste and class; and then of ethnic group. Cox offered a further perspective; he explained the everyday practice of racial categorization as an imposition that served a political function. Marxists have developed it further.

The intellectual tradition established by Park turned to the notion of racism in order to incorporate the ideological dimension to intergroup relations. Just prior to the challenges posed by the US Civil Rights movement, the present author attempted to summarize the prevailing state of sociological knowledge. He presented it as built upon three lines of research: upon the study of racism as an ideology, upon prejudice as a disposition and upon discrimination as a practice. His book offered nominalist definitions and explained variations in discrimination as the outcome of transactions between the parties, but, like the US work, it drew no sharp distinction between sociology and social policy.

That distinction is important to the issues discussed in chapter 5, where it was contended that public perceptions of black-white relations were profoundly influenced by the conception of racism advanced by Carmichael and Hamilton. Theirs was a realist definition suited to a political purpose that ignored the established legal definition of racial discrimination. Uncritical adoption of the Carmichael and Hamilton conception of racism caused confusion in the UN General Assembly and elsewhere. Several respected historians have since published histories of racism, using the word to serve their political purposes. Many sociologists now proffer only examples of what they consider racism; because they assume that its essence is evil, because they want to attack evil, and evil can take many forms, they cannot define racism. Their criticism of popular assumptions about what are perceived as policy problems can be seen as contributing to practical knowledge, but tacit assumptions that ordinary language suffices for the understanding of events and sentiments hinder the acquisition of new theoretical knowledge.

That the terms 'race', 'racism' and 'ethnic group' are employed differently in different countries should not disturb the sociologist, because they are policy words or emic constructs suited to political argument. In chapter 6, Riesman's innovatory use of the word 'ethnicity' was held to be realist in character, and therefore to be contrasted with the nominalist conception underlying Barth's arguments about the maintenance of ethnic boundaries. Glazer and Moynihan, by problematizing ethnicity rather than ethnic group, publicized a realist conception of ethnicity. Research into the ability of some townspeople in Uganda to identify co-ethnics, and the circumstances in which, as a result, they behave differently, has illustrated the need for studies in which the relevant variables can be permuted. How best may such knowledge be won in the study of industrial societies?

Chapters 6 and 7 have outlined an approach informed by the philosophy of critical rationalism. They maintain that research should start from whatever is perceived to be an interesting intellectual problem. The overarching problem in this field is that of accounting for the social significance attributed to phenotypical differences among humans, compared with that attributed to cultural characteristics such as ethnic origin and socio-economic status. Since social conditions change, this includes study of how relative significance changes or is prevented from changing. If research produces unexpected findings, they constitute a particularly valuable contribution to knowledge.

The intellectual demand for better identifiers, and the practical considerations that arise from changing circumstances, meet in the categories of the US census. The projections for 2050 have been noted (see chapter 2). The statement that 'Hispanic origins are not races' will have, one day, to be revised and brought into line with measures of ethnic origins. This will have a major effect upon popular US conceptions of race. A separate and important source of change in the near future will be the identity choices of persons with multiple ethnic origins, and the options that are open to them. Their choices will reflect their appraisals of the costs and benefits of alternative social paths. Studies in the US have shown that social ranking and access to economic and social resources are influenced by shade of skin colour as well as by the black-white division. Both whites and blacks discriminate on this basis. The US, like many other societies, observes a colour scale, often as part of a more general calculation of socio-economic status. Recent studies of the bonding and bridging forms of human capital illuminate some of the variables (like trust) and their relevance in given circumstances. The strength of one variable relative to others can be measured by the experimental permutation of preferences for association with co-ethnics.

When, in 1998, the American Association of Physical Anthropologists stated that 'there is no national, religious, linguistic or cultural group or economic class that constitutes a race', it was not announcing a discovery. There never had been any national, religious, linguistic or cultural group or economic class that constituted a race. With the benefit of hindsight, it can be seen that the same statement could have been made a hundred years earlier. It was an observation that belongs within the history of theoretical knowledge. Its truth was not manifest in 1898 because it took so long for Darwin's revolution to be completed and its nature to be understood. Since that revolution is of a technical character, even today it is understood by only a small section of the general public.

The 2002 ASA statement embodied a paradox. It acknowledged that, as a concept, race had no validity in the field in which it originated, but nevertheless advocated its continued use for data collection. It defended this position by asserting that, in the United States, race is a social construct. This response does not resolve the paradox because it does not consider the purposes of data collection and whether the methods employed are the best ones for those purposes. Was there not some alternative word or set of words that could be used in ways that did not deepen the divide? Instead of subjecting use of the word to critical scrutiny, by its reference to a social construct of race the ASA statement justified prevailing practice. Its rhetoric was suited to the policy problem of the moment.

To explain how the present situation has come about, it is necessary to acknowledge the enormous power of the ordinary language conception of 'race' in the American mind. It is thought to be 'common sense'. It is reinforced by the many circumstances in which residents in the United States are required to specify their 'race'. Seven of them were by the professor mentioned in chapter 1. There may be more. Ticking one of the options offered on a form is an easy step towards the main business. That gives the options their power. Is there any reason why such forms should not follow the census and indicate that those who wish may say that they are of more than one race? An increase in the options made available in official data collection could initiate a process leading to the dissolution of the one-drop rule, and help open a previously closed relationship.

That people answer questions on these forms is evidence of the operation of a social construct, but what is it a construct of? What should it be called? Whatever it may be, this construct is unique to the United States. It was created as an elaboration of the one-drop rule, and it may disappear in the future.

The paradox can be resolved by recognizing the distinction between practical and theoretical knowledge. Practical knowledge called for the continued collection of data on socio-economic differences. Theoretical knowledge demanded the more careful identification of the objects of study. In present circumstances it is important firstly to ascertain for what public policy purposes statistics about social differences are required, and secondly to inquire into the best ways to collect them. For the further growth of social science knowledge, the focus must be on the discovery of better explanations of human behaviour in this sphere of social life.

What we now know about race and ethnicity is a combination of practical and theoretical knowledge. While both kinds of knowledge have grown greatly since the end of World War II, theoretical knowledge might have grown better had sociologists reflected more deeply on the relation between things and words. Too often they have started their accounts by discussing the meanings of words instead of considering the purposes for which the words are used and whether they are the most appropriate words for those purposes. This is a very simple argument, but it is fundamental.

Notes

1. The italics have been added to emphasize that the words that follow about 'the role and consequences of race in primary social institutions and environments' are not intended to represent race as something which itself acts upon persons and things.
2. Joseph Agassi, *Towards an Historiography of Science* ('S-Gravenhage: Mouton; *History and Theory: Studies in the Philosophy of Science, Beiheft 2*, 1963).
3. W. Lloyd Warner and P. S. Lunt, *The Social Life of a Modern Community*, Yankee City Series, vol. 1 (New Haven: Yale University Press, 1941), 8–9.
4. See Popper's essay on 'The Logic of the Social Sciences' in *In Search of a Better World: Lectures and Essays from Thirty Years* (London: Routledge, 1994), especially the Sixth thesis, 66–67; the Tenth thesis, 69–72, can be ignored. Popper had little to say about the origin of hypotheses or about how experimentalists responded when their hypotheses were not confirmed. Thomas Kuhn's account of scientific revolutions suggested that science was most constructive when it upheld a system of popular, or 'normal', theories, even despite anomalous findings. Imre Lakatos combined Popper's adherence to empirical validity with Kuhn's appreciation for conventional consistency when he identified a 'progressive research programme' as based on a hard core of theoretical assumptions such that an apparent anomaly occasioned a problem shift rather than the abandonment of the core theory. See Imre Lakatos and Alan Musgrave (eds.), *Criticism and the Growth of Knowledge* (Cambridge: Cambridge University Press, 1970).

Select Bibliography

Agassi, Joseph. 1963. *Towards an Historiography of Science* (The Hague: Mouton; History and Theory. Studies in the Philosophy of Science, Beiheft 2, 1).
Anderson, Benedict. 1983. *Imagined Communities: Reflections of the Origin and Spread of Nationalism*. London: Verso.
Appiah, Kwame Anthony. 1992. *In My Father's House: Africa in the Philosophy of Culture*. London: Methuen.
Banton, Michael. 2002. *The International Politics of Race*. Cambridge: Polity.
———. 2010. 'The Vertical and Horizontal Dimensions of the Word Race', *Ethnicities* 10(1): 127–140.
Barkan, Elazar. 1992. *The Retreat of Scientific Racism: Changing concepts of race in Britain and the United States between two world wars*. Cambridge: Cambridge University Press.
Barth, Fredrik (ed.). 1969. *Ethnic Groups and Boundaries. The Social Organization of Culture Difference*. Oslo: Universitetsforlaget.
Berlin, Ira. 1998. *Many Thousands Gone: The First Two Centuries of Slavery in North America*. Cambridge, MA: Harvard University Press.
Biddiss, Michael (ed.). 1979. *Images of Race*. Leicester: Leicester University Press.
Bliss, Catherine. 2012. *Race Decoded: The Genomic Fight for Social Justice*. Stanford: Stanford University Press.
Bossuyt, Marc. 2000. 'Prohibition of Discrimination and the Concept of Affirmative Action', in *Bringing International Human Rights Law Home*, 93–106. New York: United Nations.
Brubaker, Rogers, et al. 2006. *Nationalist Politics and Everyday Ethnicity in a Transylvanian Town*. Princeton: Princeton University Press.
Brubaker, Rogers, and Frederick Cooper. 2000. 'Beyond Identity', *Theory and Society* 29(1): 1–47; reprinted in Rogers Brubaker, 2004, *Ethnicity Without Groups*, Cambridge, MA: Harvard University Press.
Bruun, H. H. 1972. *Science, Values and Politics in Max Weber's Methodology*. Copenhagen: Munksgaard.
Carmichael, Stokely, and Charles V. Hamilton. 1969. *Black Power: The Politics of Liberation in America*. Harmondsworth: Penguin.
Coleman, James S. 1990. *Foundations of Social Theory*. Cambridge, MA: Harvard.
Connerly, Ward. 2000. *Creating Equal: My Fight Against Race Preferences*. San Francisco: Encounter Books.
Coppel, Charles A. 1997. 'Revisiting Furnival's "plural society"', *Ethnic and Racial Studies* 20(3): 562–579.

Cox, Oliver C. 1948. *Caste, Class and Race: A Study in Social Dynamics.* New York: Monthly Review Press.

Davis, Allison, Burleigh B. Gardner and Mary Gardner. 1941. *Deep South: A Social Anthropological Study of Caste and Class.* Chicago: University of Chicago Press.

Davis, F. James. 1991. *Who Is Black?* University Park: The Pennsylvania State University Press.

Doyle, Bertram Wilbur. 1937. *The Etiquette of Race Relations in the South.* Chicago: University of Chicago Press.

Fenton, Steve. 2003. *Ethnicity.* Cambridge: Polity.

Fredrickson, George M. 1971. *The Black Image in the White Mind: The Debate on Afro-American Character and Destiny, 1817–1914.* New York: Harper.

———. 2002. *Racism: A Short History.* Princeton: Princeton University Press.

Fulbrook, Mary. 1978. 'Max Weber's "Interpretive Sociology": A comparison of conception and practice', *British Journal of Sociology* 29(1): 71–82.

Furnival, John S. 1948. *Colonial Policy and Practice: A Comparative Study of Burma and Netherlands India.* Cambridge: Cambridge University Press.

Gellner, Ernest. 1973. *Cause and Meaning in the Social Sciences,* edited by I. C. Jarvie and Joseph Agassi. London: Routledge.

Glazer, Nathan, and Daniel Patrick Moynihan (eds.). 1975. *Ethnicity: Theory and Experience.* Cambridge, MA: Harvard University Press.

Gluckman, Max. 1958. *Analysis of a Social Situation in Modern Zululand,* Rhodes-Livingstone Paper 28. Manchester: Manchester University Press.

Gross, Ariela J. 2008. *What Blood Won't Tell: A History of Race on Trial in America.* Cambridge, MA: Harvard University Press.

Habyarimana, James, et al. 2009. *Coethnicity: Diversity and the Dilemmas of Collective Action.* New York: Russell Sage Foundation.

Hersch, Joni. 2008. 'Profiling the New Immigrant Worker: The Effects of Skin Color and Height', *Journal of Labor Economics* 26(2): 345–386

Higgs, Robert. 1989. 'Black Progress and the Persistence of Racial Economic Inequalities, 1865–1940', in Steven Shulman and William Darity, Jr. (eds.), *The Question of Discrimination. Racial Inequality in the U.S. Labor Market,* 9–31. Middletown: Wesleyan University Press.

Homans, George. 1958. 'Social Behavior as Exchange', *American Journal of Sociology* 63: 597–606.

Horowitz, Donald L. 1985. *Ethnic Groups in Conflict.* Berkeley: University of California Press; updated edition, 2000.

———. 2001. *The Deadly Ethnic Riot.* Berkeley: University of California Press.

Huxley, Julian, and A. C. Haddon. 1935. *We Europeans: A Survey of Racial Problems.* London: Cape.

Jenkins, Richard. 2008. *Rethinking Ethnicity: Arguments and Explorations,* 2nd edition. London: Sage.

Johnson, Charles S. 1943. *Patterns of Negro Segregation.* New York: Harper.

Jordan, Winthrop D. 1968. *White Over Black. American Attitudes Toward the Negro, 1550–1812.* Chapel Hill: University of North Carolina Press.

Kahn, Jonathan. 2012. *Race in a Bottle: The Story of BiDil and Racialized Medicine in a Post-Genomic Age.* New York: Columbia University Press.

Kedourie, Elie. 1960. *Nationalism*. London: Hutchinson.

Krizsán, Andrea (ed.). 2001. *Ethnic Monitoring and Data Protection: The European Context*. Budapest: Central European University Press.

Kuhn, Thomas. 1962. *The Structure of Scientific Revolutions*. Chicago: Chicago University Press.

Laitin, David D. 2007. *Nations, States, and Violence*. Oxford: Oxford University Press.

Lakatos, Imre, and Alan Musgrave (eds.). 1970. *Criticism and the Growth of Knowledge*. Cambridge: Cambridge University Press.

Lancee, Bram, and Jaap Dronkers. 2011. 'Ethnic, Religious and Economic Diversity in Dutch Neighbourhoods: Explaining Quality of Contact with Neighbours, Trust in the Neighbourhood and Inter-Ethnic Trust', *Journal of Ethnic and Migration Studies* 37(4): 597–618, at 603.

Lind, Andrew W. (ed.). 1955. *Race Relations in World Perspective: Papers read at the Conference on Race Relations in World Perspective, Honolulu, 1954*. Honolulu: University of Hawaii Press.

Malešević, Siniša. 2004. *The Sociology of Ethnicity*. London: Sage.

Mayr, Ernst. 1982. *The Growth of Biological Thought: Diversity, Evolution, and Inheritance*. Cambridge, MA: Harvard University Press.

Mill, John Stuart. 1843. *A System of Logic: Ratiocinative and Inductive*. London: many editions.

Morning, Ann. 2011. *The Nature of Race: How Scientists Think and Teach About Human Difference*. Berkeley: University of California Press.

Murji, Karim, and John Solomos (eds.). 2005. *Racialization: Studies in Theory and Practice*. Cambridge: Cambridge University Press, 2005.

Myrdal, Gunnar, et al. 1969. *An American Dilemma: The Negro Problem and Modern Democracy*. New York: Harper.

Olson, Mancur. 1965. *The Logic of Collective Action: Public Goods and the Theory of Groups*. Cambridge, MA: Harvard University Press.

Park, Robert E., and Ernest W. Burgess. 1921. *Introduction to the Science of Sociology*. Chicago: University of Chicago Press.

Park, Robert Ezra. 1950. *Race and Culture*. Glencoe: The Free Press.

Popper, Karl R. 1957. *The Poverty of Historicism*. London: Routledge.

Provine, William B. 1971. *The Origins of Theoretical Population Genetics*. Chicago: University of Chicago Press.

Putnam Robert. 2007. 'E Pluribus Unum: Diversity and Community in the Twenty-first Century', *Scandinavian Political Studies* 30: 137–174.

Roberts, Dorothy. 2011. *Fatal Invention: How Science, Politics and Big Business Re-Create Race in the Twenty-first Century*. New York: New Press.

Robinson, Eugene. 2010. *Disintegration: The Splintering of Black America*. New York: Doubleday.

Saidemann, Stephen, and R. William Ayres. 2008. *For Kin or Country: Xenophobia, Nationalism, and War*. New York: Colombia University Press.

Schlee, Günther. 2013. 'Territorializing ethnicity: The imposition of a model of statehood on pastoralists in northern Kenya and southern Ethiopia', *Ethnic and Racial Studies* 36(5): 857–874.

Schramm, Katharina, David Skinner and Richard Rottenburg (eds.). 2012. *Identity Politics and the New Genetics*. New York: Berghahn Books.

Steele, Shelby. 1998. *A Dream Deferred: The Second Betrayal of Black Freedom in America*. New York: HarperCollins.

Sowell, Thomas. 1983. *The Economics and Politics of Race*. New York: Morrow.

Thernstrom, Stephan, and Abigail Thernstrom. 1997. *America in Back and White: One Nation, Indivisible*. New York: Simon & Schuster.

van den Berghe, Pierre L. 1967. *Race and Racism: A Comparative Perspective*. New York: Wiley.

———. 1981. *The Ethnic Phenomenon*. Amsterdam: Elsevier.

Varshney, Asutosh. 2002. *Ethnic Conflict and Civic Life: Hindus and Muslims in India*. New Haven: Yale University Press.

Wagley, Charles. 1952. *Race and Class in Rural Brazil*. Paris: UNESCO.

Walther, Carol S. 2014. 'Skin tone, biracial stratification and tri-racial stratification among sperm donors', *Ethnic and Racial Studies* 37(3): 517–536.

Warner, Lloyd, and P. S. Lunt. 1941. *The Social Life of a Modern Community*. New Haven: Yale University Press.

Warner, W. Lloyd, and Leo Srole. 1945. *The Social Systems of American Ethnic Groups*. New Haven: Yale University Press.

Weber, Max. *From Max Weber: Essays in Sociology*, edited by H. H. Gerth and C. Wright Mills. London: Kegan Paul

———. 1968. *Economy and Society: An Outline of Interpretive Sociology*, edited by Guenther Roth and Claus Wittich, translations by various authors. New York: Bedminster.

———. 2004. 'The "objectivity" of knowledge in social science and social policy', in *The Essential Weber: A Reader*, edited by Sam Whimster. London: Routledge.

Williams, Walter E. 2001. *Race and Economics: How much can be blamed on discrimination?* Stanford: Hoover Institution publication 599.

Wilson, William Julius. 1978. *The Declining Significance of Race: Blacks and Changing American Institutions*. Chicago: University of Chicago Press.

Wimmer, Andreas. 2013. *Ethnic Boundary Making: Institutions, Power, Networks*. Oxford: Oxford University Press.

Wrong, Dennis H. 1961. 'The Oversocialized Conception of Man in Modern Sociology', *American Sociological Review* 26(2): 183–193.

Index of Names

Index of Subjects